D1514774

Oliver Twist

Oliver Twist

THE OFFICIAL COMPANION TO THE ITV DRAMA SERIES

TOM McGREGOR

OLIVER TWIST

A Diplomat Films production for HTV in association with United Productions and WGBH/Boston.

© HTV Ltd, MCMXCIX.

CAST LIST

Oliver Twist	Sam Smith
Mr Bumble	David Ross
Mrs Mann	Julie Walters
Edwin Leeford	Tim Dutton
Monks	Marc Warren
Mr Brownlow	Michael Kitchen
Elizabeth Leeford	Lindsay Duncan
Fagin	Robert Lindsay
Bill Sikes	Andy Serkis
Nancy	Emily Woof
Artful Dodger	Alex Crowley
Charley Bates	Roland Manookian
Bet	Isla Fisher
Mrs Bedwin	Annette Crosbie
Mr Grimwig	John Grillo
Sally	Liz Smith
Mr Sowerberry	Roger Lloyd Pack
Mrs Sowerberry	Ger Ryan
Noah Claypole	James Bradshaw
Charlotte	Tracey Murphy
Agnes Fleming	Sophia Myles
Mr Fleming	Alun Armstrong
Rose Fleming (aged 7)	Charlotte Lamont Fisher
Rose Fleming (aged 17)	Keira Knightly
Doctor Losberne	David Bark-Jones
Brittles	Morgan Jones
Giles	Sam Kelly
Toby Crackitt	Andrew Schofield
Mrs Corney	Rosalind March
Doctor Butchard	Michael Bertenshaw
James Matthews	Simon Kunz
Blacksmith	Callum McPherson
Woodcroft (stable lad)	Iain Robertson
Richard Leeford	John Quarmby
Scottish Lawyer – Mr Ferguson	Clive Russell
Italian Doctor	Jacob Shwartz
Fleming's Maid	Rachel Stanton
Bookseller	Colin Higgins
Great Lubberly Fellow	Jonathan Owen
Policeman	Daniel Brown
Chairman	Zdenek Maryska
Mr Fang	David Ryall
Clerk of the Court	Geoffrey Larder
Mr Temple	Ian Taylor
First Old Woman	Angela Vale
Second Old Woman	Ysanne Churchman
Third Old Woman	Marlene Sidaway
Second Man	Edward Woodall
First Man	Phil Kavanagh
Doctor Critchley	Richard Howard
Beggar Woman	Joy Harrison
Vigil Keeper	Cathy Murphy
Workhouse Nurse	Andrea Miltner
First Twin	Deborah Vale
Second Twin	Tessa Vale
Waiting Mother	Elizabeth Wharton
Mr Slout	Frantisek Nedved
Limkins	David Foxxe
Finders	Desmond Barritt
Board Clerk	Daniel Brocklebank
Gruff But Kindly Man	Robert Russell
Sick Patient	Laura Zam
First Board Man	Richard Syms
Second Board Man	Ken Parry
Elderly Vicar	Hugh Lloyd
First Boy	Nicholas Connell
Tall Lad	Michael Nickless
Small Boy	Thomas McEnchroe
Boy at Fagin's Door	Tom Langley
Boy Outside Fagin's Door	Sasha Frost
Griefstruck Mother	Vivienne Burgess
Grieving Husband	Paul Leonard
Clergyman	Doug Fisher
Vestry Clerk	Howard Karloff
Female Pauper	Hilary Sesta
Doctor's Young Apprentice	John Comer
Homely Maid	Sarah Flind
Chertsey Cook	Annette Badland
Chertsey Housemaid	Laura Grace Cockroft
Young Artful Dodger	Ollie Peel
Young Nancy	Zuzana Krausova
First Workhouse Boy	Luke Atherton
First Drinker	Jonathan Jaynes
Second Drinker	Arthur Kelly
Pedlar	Alan Pentony
Passing Policeman	Craster Pringle
First Warden	Rich Gold
Second Warden	Robert Orr
Turnkey	Ricky Glover
Irish Assistant	Maria Doyle Kennedy
Cart Driver	Steve Jarman
Carriage Driver	John Peacock/Les Mayon
Grimwig's Clerk	Derek Bohan
Teetotal Girl	Lisa Marie Gravell
Early Riser	Phil Kavanagh
First Crowd Member	David O'Kelly
Kindly Policeman	Sebastian Abinieri
Well-Dressed Man	Alex McAvoy
Wounded Man	Ron Webster
Brownlow's Footman	Julius Krajewsky
Brownlow's Coachman	Hayden Webb
Stunt Co-ordinators	Gareth Milne
	Gabe Connelly

UK CREW

Director	Renny Rye
Producer	Keith Thompson
Executive Producers	Alan Bleasdale
	Michele Buck
	Rebecca Eaton
	WGBH/Boston
Line Producer	Alison Barnett
Music composed by	Elvis Costello
	Paul Pritchard
Casting	Ros and John Hubbard
Casting Assistant	Abbi Harris
Script Associate	Katharine Norbury
Script Supervisor	Sam Donovan
1st Assistant Director	Peter Freeman
2nd Assistant Director	Jeff Taylor
3rd Assistant Director	Fletcher Rodley
Floor Runners	Mitch Skinner
	Gareth Thomas
Location Manager	Jane Soans
Unit Managers	Martin Joy
	Mally Chung
	Rachel Neale
Production Accountant	Guy Barker
Assistant Accountant	Nicky Coats
Production Coordinator	Sara Hamil
Assistant Prod. Coordinator	Liza Carmel
Production Secretary	Emily Bullock
Production Runners	Nicky Waltham
	Jonathan Mead
Production Designer	Malcolm Thornton
Art Director	Stevie Herbert
Assistant Art Directors	Adam Marshall
	Clara Morland
Production Buyer	Gill Farr
Assistant Production Buyers	Shelley Pond
	Sophie Tyler
Props Master	Gary Watson
Standby Props	Danny Euston
	Mark Bevan
Dressing Props	Steve Smith
	Demsey Cook
Storeman	Micky Cox
Construction Manager	Dave Creed
Carpenters	Paul Beeson
	Darren Caen
	Steve Protheroe
Painter	Kevin Biggs
Standby Painter	Jim Fennesy
Standby Carpenter	Laurie Griffiths
Standby Rigger	Charlie Macher
Standby Stagehand	Stephen Macher
Costume Designer	Ros Ebbutt
Make-up Designer	Lesley Lamont-Fisher
Wardrobe Supervisor	Michael Skorepa
Wardrobe Design Assistant	Amanda Keable
Wardrobe Assistant	Donna Nicholls
Wardrobe Dailies	Marie Ross
	Ray Greenhill
	Sharon Gillham
Make-up Artist	Chris Redman
Make-up Dailies	Lynne Butterworth
	Derek Lloyd
	Hannah Cole
	Nikita Way
Director of Photography	Walter McGill
Camera Operator	Steve Alcorn
Focus Puller	Christian Abomnes
Clapper Loader	John Priddle
Grips	Dave Logan
	Rupert Lloyd-Parry
Camera Trainee	Billy Charlton
Gaffer	Geoff Healy
Best Boy	Phil Reader
Electricians	Graham Newton
	David Campbell
	Martin Trevis
Sound Recordist	Kate Morath
Boom Operator	Sarah Morton
Dubbing Mixer	Ian Tapp
Sound Trainee	Simon Webster
Dubbing Editor	John Downer
Editors	David Rees
	Wendy Edgar Jones
Post Production Supervisor	Alasdair Whitelaw
Assistant Editor	Tom Kinnersly
Post Production Assistant	Sara Chapman
Magic Consultant	Ali Bongo
SFX Co-ordinator	Colin Gorry
Visual Effects Supervisor	Dennis Lowe
Horse Masters	Steve Dent
	Lex and Jane Ruddiman
Stunt Coordinators	Gareth Milne
	Gabe Cronelly
Publicity	Kirwin Milard Associates
Stills Photographer	Nobby Clark

Medical Advisor	Malcolm Holt
Unit Nurse	Terri Sheed
Stand ins	Steve Ricard
	Kim Taylor
Catering	Woodhall Catering
Unit Drivers	Simon Barker
	Benjamin Hanny
	Fergus Cotter
	Steve Rogers
	Terry Bleasdale
	Christopher Billings
Facility Drivers	Charlie Simpson
	Frank Carr
	Simon Pickering
	Bill Clare
	Nick Donnelly

CZECH CREW

Executive company	Czech-Anglo Productions s.r.o.
Producer	Kevan Van Thompson
Production Manager	Pavel Nový
Unit Manager	Zybněk Pippal
Location Manager	Jaroslav Vaculík
Assistant Location Manager	Daniela Bužgová
Assistant Prod. Coordinator	Tim Gorman
Production Assistant	Martina Burgetová
Production Secretary	Monika Machytková
Set Interpreter	Věra Koháková
Production Accountant	Lenka Jandová
Assistant Accountant	Jessica Stoltz
Cashier	Petr Čermák
1st Assistant Director	Tomáš Zelenka
3rd Assistant Director	Lenka Pavláková
	Roman Fara
Customs	Pavel Lehotský
Unit Nurse	Tomáš Kos
Runners	Lukáš Pospíšil
	Lucie Pokorná
Casting	Nancy Bishop
	Lenka Horacková
	Martina Kubešová
Gaffer	Milan Jirsa
Best Boy	Martin Rain
Electricians	Miroslav Vojkůvka
	Ivan Ksandr
	Jaromir Šimek
Clapper Loader	Vladimír Duben
Video Operator	Oto Matějka
Steadicam	Jaromir Šedina
	Jiří Zavřel
Grips	Petr Bautz
	Vladimír Bursík
Sound Assistant	Richard Fischer
Wardrobe Assistants	Petra Barochová
	Šarka Zvolenská
Make-up Assistants	Zdeněk Klika
	Ivana Langhammerová
Make-up and Costume Interp.	Martina Götthansová
Art Director	Martin Malý
Assistant Art Director	Linda Jabloň
Art Department Interpreter	Štěpánka Ročková
Props Buyer	Olga Rosenfelderová
Construction Manager	Jiří Prchal
Construction Standbys	Jiří Pocta
	Jiří Fišar
Props master	Jaroslav Cesal
Storeman	Stanislav Lukšan
Standby Props	Radan Kapinos
	Marek Šima
Dressing Props	Jan Gál
	Martin Tlamicha
Stills photographer	Zdeněk Vávra
Filmka Stunts	Ladislav Lahoda
	Dimo Lipitkovský
	Jindrich Klaus
Horsemaster	Pavel Vokoun
Flash Barrandov – special effects	Jaroslav Štolba
	Martin Oberlander
	Petr Michalicka
	Jiří Vojtech
	Petr Lukavec
Catering	Jan Srbený
	Jiří Lindner
	Karel Bláha
	Jaroslav Mácek
Base Camp	Martin Stanek
	Karek Mach
	Miloš Hobi
Drivers	Jiří Beran
	Josef Ferki
	Josef Havlíček
	Ondrej Hůla
	Josef Kuska
	Jan Kuželík
	František Rys
	Karel Šterba
	Jaroslav Zátka
	Josef Komárek
	Zdeněk Suchý
	Vratislav Voščka
	Karel Krejč

ACKNOWLEDGEMENTS

Diplomat Films Ltd wishes to acknowledge the following individuals and organisations for their help in the making of *Oliver Twist*.

Ros Hubbard, John Hubbard and Abbi Harris of Hubbard Casting
Marylyn Phillips of the Jackie Palmer Agency
Alan and Jill Smith
Czech-Anglo Productions, Prague
CSA Czech Airlines
The residents of Alston, Cumbria
Barrandov Studios, Prague

First Published in Great Britain in 1999 by Virgin Publishing Ltd
Thames Wharf Studios
Rainville Road
London W6 9HA

A catalogue record for this book is available from the British Library.

ISBN 1 85227 837 4

Design
Town Group Creative, London

Photographs
Nobby Clark (Copyright © 1999 HTV Ltd): pages 1–5; 30; 40; 47; 58–62; 68–72; 76; 80–118; 120–131; 133–155
Mary Evans Picture Library: pages 5–22; 26; 80; 156–160
Hulton Getty: pages 24; 26
Simon Danby: pages 32–39
Zdenek Vávra: pages 42–45; 50–51; 54; 56; 63–64; 79; 99; 119; 121; 132
Graeme Grant: pages 53; 54; 67

UNITED
productions

Contents

The Big Boys' Playground

Charles Dickens
1812 - 1870
W. Reynolds

One person alone is the reason for my dramatisation of *Oliver Twist* and this delightful and evocative book by 'Tom McGregor', for there would have been nothing at all to adapt, structure, create or illustrate without the pervading genius of Charles Dickens. During his hurtling life he wrote more masterpieces than any other novelist who has ever lived, with a vividness that transcends generations and centuries.

Original greatness and a depth of humanity, both within the text and the author, have two effects upon the fool who dares to dramatise a classic. Well, they certainly did this fool!

Initially, I was very happy, confident even, because any novel of Dickens has characters, dialogue, set-pieces, comedy and tragedy in abundance...and then suddenly I was terrified. Not worried you understand. Not scared. Not even really really frightened. *Terrified.* For I had realised, after my immediate elation, that I was about to enter the same playground as Charles Dickens. The big boys' playground. And I didn't feel very big at all.

For nearly two months I walked around the huge forbidding walls of this playground, day in day out, night after night, trying to find the entrance. I was even more haunted by the fear that if I ever did find the way in, my path would be blocked by a glowering gang led by Shakespeare, Tolstoy, Joyce, Beckett and Sophocles, muttering, 'Don't let him in, Charles; he isn't a big boy. He isn't even tall for his age.'

Of course, I never got into that playground, not even temporarily, but finally I found a way of climbing the wall and looking over the top. And, again, as always, I had Charles Dickens to thank.

He, however, might not have wanted to thank me on this or any other occasion, for the only way I could begin my task and make sense of the structure of the novel was to attack one of the very few weaknesses in *Oliver Twist*.

The weakness lies, in my genuinely humble opinion, in that Dickens was making the plot up as he went along, chapter by chapter, in monthly instalments for a magazine. He was also a remarkably young man, attempting his first format novel. Like almost every writer, of any age, he wouldn't have had a clear picture, when he started his journey, where his travels would take him and where his final destination was to be. Naturally, writing in this manner, with no opportunity to revise text before the next instalment date or produce a second draft, it is clear that near the end Dickens painted himself and his plot into quite a desperate and multi-coloured corner.

Consequently, for several pages in Chapter 51, he spectacularly introduces not only several characters from the past, but also traumatic events leading to the very start of the book – the birth in the workhouse of Oliver Twist.

And in those few pages, Dickens cavalierly produces and then casually dismisses the most remarkable, indeed fabulous, collection of minor characters. We meet, albeit second-hand, and for the first and last time, Edwin Leeford, the father of Oliver Twist; Mrs Leeford, the wicked witch of a wife of Edwin Leeford; Agnes Fleming, the haunted young mother of Oliver Twist, and her loving but broken father, the retired sea captain, Mr Fleming. And it is also here, in Chapter 51, that he explains, finally, Monks' mad and lurking pursuit of his half brother, Oliver Twist.

So, it was there where I found my way of attempting to tell this story. 'In his end is my beginning', as someone else from the big boys playground once almost said. Take the wonderful story that Dickens threw away, discarded like a paintbrush in a corner, and tell that story to start with.

And then, maybe, small boy, not very tall for your age, you will have the courage to stay on the wall and begin to capture and clarify the adventures of Brownlow and Fagin, Bill Sikes and Nancy, and a baby born as his mother lies dying...

Finally this, of course, is not my book to dedicate to anyone, but I must not miss this opportunity to thank our director, Renny Rye, for his brilliant determination; his magnificent company and crew; our line producer, Alison Barnett and her team, for pulling us through thick and thin; Ros Hubbard and all at Hubbard Casting, for their knowledge, divine interventions, support and suppers; my researcher and mentor and rescuer of lost causes, Katherine Norbury; my wife, Julie, for staying there through my despair, and last but far from least, Keith Thompson, my business partner and producer at Diplomat Films, and his wife Dawn, for their patience and guidance when the fax started ringing at five in the morning. Every morning. Some mornings, there would be twenty pages of script, but other mornings there would be one page containing one word. 'Help!'

Alan Bleasdale
July 1999

What if

Nothing w

... And then I come back. I'm n

Yes. It will. ◆ ◆

Mourn... Weep? Howl?

For as soon as we can,

Retreat to one room

And we will live happil

in your darkened mansi

(SHE LOOKS AT H

with your wedding dress

I am older than you. A

and your memories.

You have me mistaken

And then what will I do with the rest

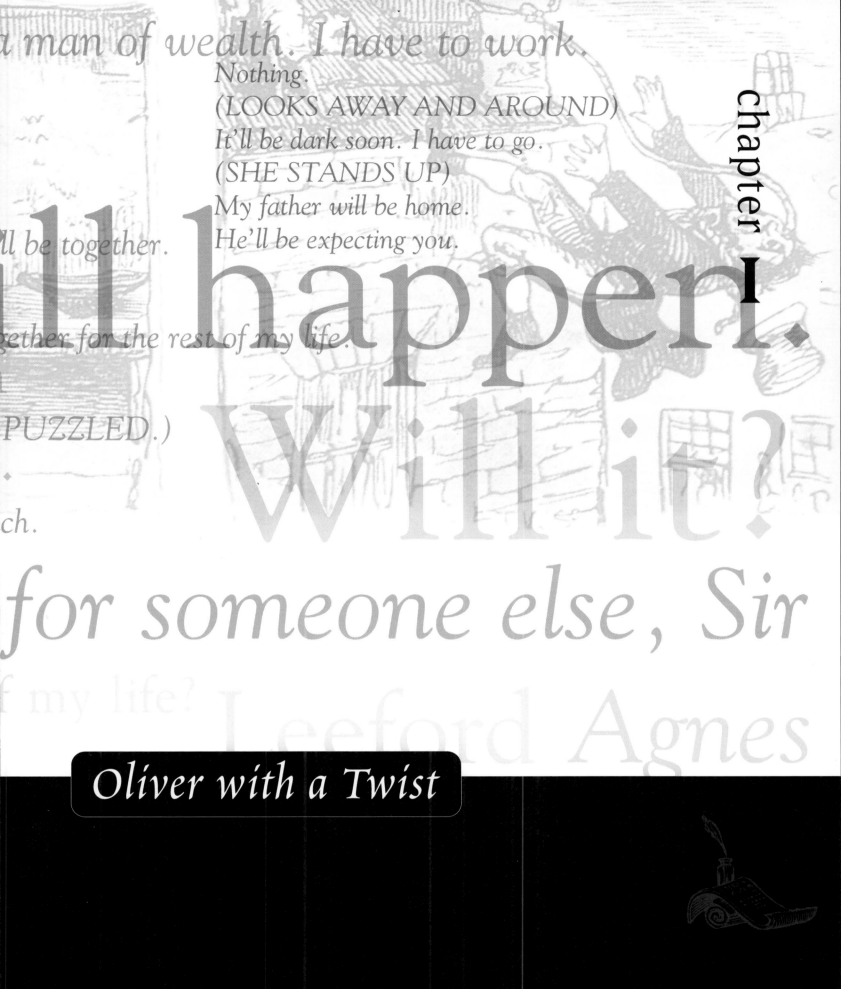

a man of wealth. I have to work.
Nothing.
(LOOKS AWAY AND AROUND)
It'll be dark soon. I have to go.
(SHE STANDS UP)
My father will be home.
He'll be expecting you.

ll be together.

ll happen.

ether for the rest of my life.

PUZZLED.)

Will it?

ch.

for someone else, Sir

f my life? Leeford Agnes

chapter I

Oliver with a Twist

When first published in 1837, Oliver Twist appeared with these now well-known illustrations by George Cruickshank. This was his impression of what was to become one of the most famous scenes in fiction – Oliver asks for more.

There is a letter from Alan Bleasdale to his researcher and editor Kate Norbury, dated 15 August 1998, that ends with the words 'I have to leave Rome tonight!' The exclamation is not one of glee but of gloom: the letter began with a vaguely grumpy 'I only worked until three o'clock yesterday morning, because I got stuck.'

The next epistle to Kate, dated the same night, begins ominously. 'I am not going to leave Rome tonight…' It then runs to three pages of explanation as to why his departure has been delayed. But at least it ends on a happier note: 'I'm going to watch *Match of the Day* and go to bed. I'm also going to have a choc-ice, but you don't need to know that.'

However, the reader needs to know what's going on. Alan Bleasdale isn't in Rome (no *Match of the Day* there); he's in Liverpool, and the only journey he's making is one that goes round in circles. The problem is the murder of Leeford by his wife and the whereabouts of his will; the document that holds the key to the entire plot of *Oliver Twist*. Viewers will see no problem – there isn't one now – but in the beginning things were different. And they were partially resolved by lengthy responses from Kate Norbury that contained, amongst other things, details of the 1820s procedure of transferring wills from one place to another; a breakdown of how Mrs Leeford and Monks would have journeyed to Rome and back; descriptions of Rome spas in that era (Leeford's Uncle Richard dies in one), and a list of poisons that Mrs Leeford could have obtained without arousing suspicion. She chose prussic acid – but she would have had the option of buying oxalic acid, powdered jolap, laudanum or arsenic. All were sold in 2oz packets over the counter.

left: Noah Claypole, the undertaker's chief apprentice. He feels himself greatly superior to the orphaned Oliver as, in Dickens' words, 'he could trace his genealogy all the way back to his parents'.

right: The Artful Dodger introduces Oliver to the 'respectable old gentleman' – Fagin.

All of the above revolves round a scenario that, in the final draft, runs to eight pages of script.

There are 447 pages of script in this adaptation; and each one is the product of acres of paper, months of research, endless queries and detailed responses. They make for a fascinating insight into the working methods of one of Britain's greatest TV writers. Alan Bleasdale may claim that he isn't qualified to join the Big Boys in their playground, but he certainly did his homework. Yet, typically, he claims no credit. 'I'd like it to be made *absolutely certain* that I couldn't have done it without Kate.'

At that stage, no-one at ITV, United Productions or WGBH Boston knew exactly *what* he was doing. Diplomat Films – the partnership run by Keith Thompson and Alan Bleasdale – had been commissioned to write and produce the new *Oliver Twist*, but the other parties involved hadn't a clue exactly how new this version was going to be. It isn't – by Dickens' standards – a very long book, and Michele Buck, Controller of Drama at United, was thinking along the lines of a four-hour drama. 'Alan and Keith said seven,' she recalls with a smile. 'I was horrified. I tried to tell them it was a *short* book. They wouldn't listen, of course. Alan said "trust me and then we'll talk about it". Next thing I knew Alan was on the phone saying that he'd written the first two hours and was feeling pretty confident about them.' (This, of course, was several months, a fair smattering of *angst* and an impressive pile of research notes later.)

'When he told me that Oliver wasn't born until the end of the second hour I laughed. Then I read the script.' All traces of amusement disappear as Michele Buck recalls her reaction to the first two hours. 'It was stunning; the most engrossing script I've ever read. It's a *Romeo and Juliet*; it's star-crossed lovers...and of course it makes absolute sense. Alan's taken a few pages from the end of the book – he hasn't actually *invented* these people – and has explained how Oliver came to be a Workhouse orphan, and why people are after him. This,' she adds with vehemence, 'is going to be the definitive *Oliver Twist*.'

And it's not just because of the script. The whole look of this piece is different. As Keith Thompson says, 'I was absolutely determined that there should be a really strong look to it. A very strong visual style with lots of blackness and filth, *real* filth – set against the vibrant colour of the world of the Leefords and Brownlow. For me, the best Dickens' adaptations with regard to the look have been the David Lean film and the BBC's *Bleak House* [starring Diana Rigg]. One doesn't want to emulate Lean or copy *Bleak House*, but they successfully showed the importance of the look.' Keith would no doubt be heartened to hear Robert Lindsay's (unsolicited) comments on that. 'The real brilliance of this production is the comparison of wealth and abject poverty...the serious wealth of the Leefords in London and Rome with these palatial houses, and then these people in Fagin's world. They lived like *rats*. I mean, the abject squalor...' Robert Lindsay (Fagin) trails into a disbelieving silence. Or perhaps it's a slightly peeved silence. The production crew don't pull any punches when it comes to rat-like squalor. They don't just give an impression of filth in Fagin's den. They deliver the real McCoy – and this writer has a dry-cleaning bill to prove it.

But Fagin. It's always Fagin. Mention *Oliver Twist* and you get Fagin. And Fagin, for Alan Bleasdale, was a problem. 'There are some really horrible things in this book,' he says with feeling. 'And the constant, merciless, *upsetting* use of the word "Jew" was one of them. I couldn't go with that.' Then he pauses and looks, momentarily, extremely fierce. 'If this production is going to be what everyone – especially me – wants it to be, I don't want it to look as if I've done something that will upset the memory of one of the greatest writers of all time. When I took liberties I took them in the hope that he would understand, and that the people who are part of the Dickens Appreciation Society will understand.'

Forget the ferocity. It's not that at all. It's just something unfamiliar to a lot of British people. It's passion. And it can be found throughout the entire script – and all the way through Alan Bleasdale's research notes. Here's a note he wrote to himself: 'Be brutal with chunks [of plot] that don't work to rejoice in the best of Dickens' work.' It's a fleeting scribble, an *aide memoire*, and it's not there for posterity. It lurks amongst other scribbles (half of which, if truth be told, are completely illegible). Alan Bleasdale gave this writer unrestricted access to his notes, and many of them are more pertinent to the plot than that. But who, other than a passionate person (or a writer of hymns, but that's probably the same thing), would use the word 'rejoice'?

'Well, you see, Alan's mad,' says Lindsay Duncan. She's referring to the fact that Alan Bleasdale wrote the part of Mrs Leeford with Lindsay in mind – and wasn't going to take 'no' for an answer (see page 106). Then she elucidates on the method behind that madness. 'He has this extraordinary, vivid, wild, *glorious* imagination – but it's always anchored in truth.'

opposite: Sikes with his companion Bullseye. Like every other actor, the canine thespian playing the part in this dramatisation had to go into make-up before his scenes were filmed. Scars were applied to his face and torso and his glowingly healthy coat was dusted down.

right: Oliver in the pleasant environs of Mr Brownlow's country house. Here, Dickens describes him imagining in his sleep, and with 'a glow of terror', that he's back in Fagin's den. But the nightmare is near to reality – he wakes to find Fagin and Monks at the window.

On a very personal level, there is truth behind the character of Monks. 'If you want to know the honest truth,' says Alan, 'once I'd got over the excitement of *Oliver Twist* and having the opportunity to do something I've wanted to do for twenty-five years...after I'd got over the worries about the Jewishness and the sentimentality and the ludicrous coincidences of the plot, the one thing that kept me going was the character of Monks. Because of my son.'

Eighteen years ago one of Alan Bleasdale's sons developed epilepsy, and it's something Alan has always wanted to write about. Gooey sentimentality is never his way, and it's interesting that he's kept the sinister aspect of the character as well. He looks, in fact, *extremely* sinister. Marc Warren, who plays him, says that 'people are wary of talking to me when I'm in character'. But this Monks is not the shadowy, and rather unsatisfactory anti-hero of Dickens. Alan Bleasdale is quite adamant about that. 'I refuse to make Monks the anti-hero of this piece. You've got to remember that part of the thing in Dickens' time was melodrama – and Monks is very melodramatic. Because of our son, I was determined not just to make him someone who falls down and has fits.' And, perhaps crucially, the character is ultimately defined by his morality rather than his physicality. There's a scribble on the research notes that reads, 'Monks – broken and imperfect, but not guilty.'

left: Rose takes Oliver to visit the tablet (there is no coffin) that marks his mother's tomb. The very last page of *Oliver Twist* is, curiously, written in the first person, and Dickens writes...'if the spirits of the Dead ever come back to earth, to visit spots hallowed by the love – the love beyond the grave – of those they knew in life, I believe that the shade of Agnes sometimes hovers round that solemn nook.'

opposite: Fagin in his death-cell. Dickens writes that 'The condemned criminal was seated on his bed, rocking himself from side to side, with a countenance more like that of a snared beast than the face of a man.'

'I have an absolute moral compunction to show that if you do something really bad,' says Alan Bleasdale, 'there will be a consequence to it. There are bad consequences all the way through this, but not for Monks. I can't remember the last time I felt so good about writing a character.'

The word 'writing' is, to some extent, a misnomer. Alan Bleasdale damaged his back – badly – half-way through the process of penning the script. He was in hospital for three-and-a-half weeks and, once home, couldn't even sit at his desk. 'For the first and only time in my life I had to dictate. I had no option, timewise. The last three hours were dictated to Kate with me lying on the couch like Barbara Cartland.'

That retrospective remark makes it all sound rather jolly. It was quite the opposite. Writers will always agonise about *what* they write; rarely are they forced to address *how* they write. 'I had no idea until then – I simply hadn't realised – that I've always said every word of dialogue out loud to myself. You don't understand the process you go through; you just sit there alone in a room.' And Alan Bleasdale usually sits alone in his room until the wee small hours, or right through the night.

Enter Kate Norbury. She had already been researching and editing the script for four months and the pair had established an excellent working relationship. 'I couldn't have got a secretary,' recalls Alan. 'Nobody hired for the job would have been prepared to sit there until three in the morning. And I *had* to have someone who I knew. But it must have been slightly terrifying for Kate. I'm a method writer – I *become* the people in the script – and there are events and scenes in the last two hours that are on the edge of madness. Kate had to live through that.' In the light of his discovery about his methods, a comment of Lindsay Duncan echoes with particular resonance. 'He invests imaginatively to such a degree...he believes so completely in the characters. I think he must act out the whole thing in his head.'

This is beginning to sound like a press release about Alan Bleasdale. Maybe that's no bad thing (he certainly wouldn't write one himself), but the script of *Oliver Twist* would still be lying on his desk were it not for the input of scores of other talented people. The unsung heroes of the TV industry – the people who bring script to screen.

Flash houses: pubs such as the Three Cripples. Exclusively
used by criminals, juvenile pickpockets and prostitutes.
Flimps: pickpockets who operated, lightning quick, in crowds.
Smatter hauling: stealing handkerchiefs.

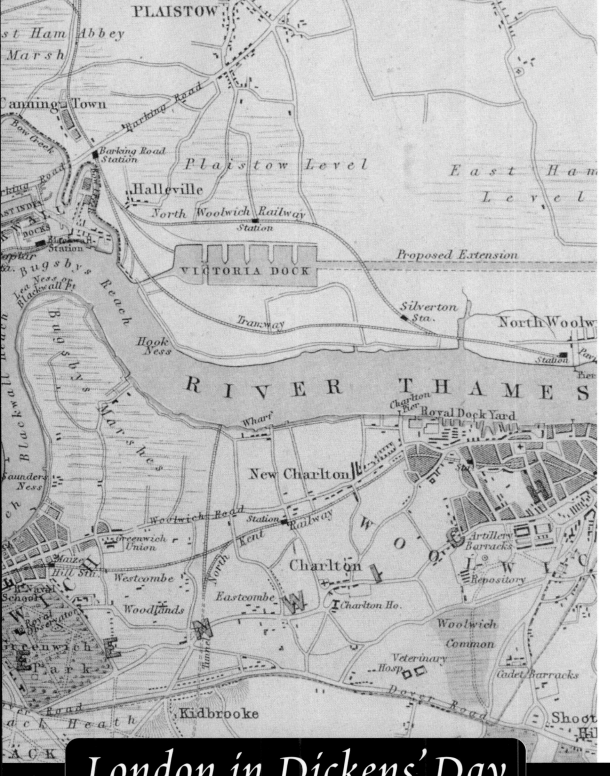

London in Dickens' Day

Flash Houses, Flimps and Smatter Hauling[1]

LOWEST LIFE in LONDON. Tom, Jerry and Logic, among the unsophisticated Sons and Daughters of Nature, at All Max in the East.

Dubious east end drinking establishment
c.1820. George Cruickshank.

The Three Cripples bar featured in Oliver Twist would have been even more dubious than this. It's described in Alan Bleasdale's stage directions as 'full of drunken grotesques, a fog of tobacco smoke, a pianist "with a bluish nose, and his face tied up for the benefit of the toothache" (Dickens), several inebriated women singers waiting in line, including Nancy and Bet; the manager of The Three Cripples, known as the Chairman, and the vast majority of the customers are frighteningly young. There is no tomorrow in this place.'

Oliver Twist was roundly criticised in some quarters for its depiction of a world many people would rather not have known about. Yet Dickens was, and remained, unrepentant about immersing his readers in the underbelly of society. Twenty years after the first publication of the novel, he explained his motives for doing so:

I had read of thieves by the scores; seductive fellows (amiable for the most part), faultless in dress, plump in pocket, choice in horse-flesh, bold in bearing, fortunate in gallantry, great at a song [anyone remember 'Oom Pah Pah'?] a bottle, pack of cards or dice-box, and fit companions for the bravest. But I had never met (except in Hogarth) with the miserable reality. It appeared to me that to draw a knot of such associates in crime as really did exist; to paint them in all their deformity, in all their wretchedness, in all the squalid misery of their lives; to show them as they really are, for ever skulking uneasily through the dirtiest paths of life, with the great black ghastly gallows closing up their prospect, turn them where they might; it appeared to me that to do this, would be to attempt a something which was needed, and which would be a service to society. And therefore I did it as best I could.

He did a thoroughly good job. His narrative largely takes place in a grotesque Babylon teeming with misery and horror – and *Oliver Twist* has been described as 'the greatest fictional representation of the underworld' (Kellew Chesney, *The Victorian Underworld*). It may be a work of fiction, but the backdrop is factual. Facts which were extremely unpalatable. And, to today's audiences, almost unimaginable.

An extract from The *London Journal* in 1840, for example, describes the plight of the poor – the sort of people whom Oliver, newly apprenticed to Sowerberry the undertaker, would have encountered:

> *Imagine men, women, children, all barefooted, ploughing through the nasty, filthy mire. Some were leaning against the wall for lack of a place to sit, others were squatting on the ground, there were children lying about in the mud like pigs... I saw children without a stitch of clothing, young girls, nursing mothers with no shoes on their feet, wearing only a tattered shift which barely covered their naked bodies... Inside and out the decrepit hovels are like the rags of the people who live in them. Neither the windows nor the doors of most of these lodgings can be closed off; floors are mostly bare earth... everyone sleeps in the one room, father, mother, sons, daughters and friends, like so many animals.*

On the sliding scale of slums, those would not have been the worst. At the bottom of the barrel was Jacob's Island, where Dickens has Fagin establishing his second den. Known as the 'Venice of Drains', it was a putrefying backwater in Bermondsey almost exclusively inhabited by the criminal classes. Charles Knight, in *Passages of a Working Life*, his acclaimed exploration of Victorian London, wrote that:

> *Whoever ventures here finds the streets, by courtesy so called, thronged with loiterers, and sees, through half-glazed windows, rooms crowded to suffocation. The stagnant gutters in the middle of the lanes, the filth choking up the dark passages which open up onto the highways, all these scarce leave so dispiriting an impression on the passenger as the condition of the houses. Walls the colour of bleached soot, doors falling from their hinges, door-posts worm eaten, windows where shivered panes of glass alternate with wisps of straw, old hats and lumps of bed-ticken or brown paper, bespeak the last and frailest shelter than can be interposed between man and the elements.*

Knight goes on to describe the warren of galleries and walkways connecting the buildings, which served as perfect escape routes from any police foolish enough to venture into Jacob's Island.

All very grim – and Dickens' own description of the area tallies exactly. In Chapter 50 of *Oliver Twist*, his 'establishing shot' describes the area as 'the filthiest, the strangest, the most extraordinary of the many localities that are hidden in London, wholly unknown, even by name, to the great mass of its inhabitants.'

Difficult to imagine now, and impossible to envisage how a TV production team could recreate anything approaching such conditions. But they did – smack in the heart of the glittering jewel in the crown of the Czech Republic. They filmed the Jacob's Island scenes in a town called Chesky Krumlov: possibly the most beautiful and perfectly preserved medieval town in Central Europe.

But if film – for its own strange, celluloid reasons – is obliged to tamper with the truth, Dickens was doing just the opposite. One of the sharpest axes he had to grind in *Oliver Twist* was against the Poor Law Amendment Act of 1834, which cast the monstrous black shadow of the Workhouse over countless lives. The Act was supposedly designed for the benefit of those who couldn't support themselves: outdoor relief was, for the most part, abolished, and paupers were admitted to a Workhouse instead. In practice, this meant 'out of sight, out of mind'.

London slum scene
Field Lane, Holborn c.1840.
Artist unknown
Note business premises of
Fagin and Scrooge.

opposite: in stark contrast to the squalor of Fagin's world, the Workhouses of the day were spotless; the female inmates' only occupation was to scrub and clean. Note the 'No Smoking' sign. It refers to pipes – cigarettes were as yet unknown.

Conditions in the Workhouses were deliberately made to be as unpleasant as possible to discourage the 'idle poor' from benefiting from the insitution. Anyone even remotely able-bodied would go to enormous lengths to avoid being admitted, and people would endure appalling cold and hunger before applying to the Workhouse. Here's why: husbands and wives were separated from each other and their children; everyone was required to eat (mainly inadequate amounts of gruel, broth, potatoes and bread) in absolute silence; visitors were banned except by special permission and the ill, the pregnant and the insane were lodged, often indiscriminately, in tiny cots crammed together. Infants would be moved out to Baby Farms – establishments created to reduce the mortality rate amongst paupers. They would stay in the farms until they were six (as opposed to Oliver's grand old age of ten), when they were either apprenticed or returned to their local workhouse. If, that is, they survived the farm. Mortality rates in rural areas were around 60 per cent. In towns they were as high as 90 per cent.

Life in Workhouses was, in theory, dominated by... work. Women cleaned, scrubbed, made and washed uniforms (Workhouses, unsurprisingly, were spotlessly clean), whilst men generally broke stone or picked oakum. Or rather, they would have if they were capable of work. In 1841, Portsea Workhouse lodged 725 souls. Only twelve of them were able-bodied. (Apologies to the blameless town of Alston in Cumbria. It provided the exterior of the Workhouse where Oliver was born and suffered some of his greatest indignities. The interior, spookily, was filmed in a monastery near Prague.)

English Factory Slaves. Pl.3 Their daily employment. —

Documentation of the horrors child workers had to endure c.1835. George Cruickshank

In Dickens' original, Oliver was almost apprenticed to a chimney-sweep – a trade notorious for misconduct and brutality. Abuse from their masters was rife; terrified urchins were driven up chimneys by having their feet scorched. They also risked serious accident, respiratory disease and, apparently, cancer of the groin.

Outwith the Workhouse, and before Fagin's gang decamped for the brutal finale at Jacob's Island, the people with whom Dickens largely concerns himself are the 'dangerous classes' of the era. Thieves, bullies, beggars, touts and tarts, they would probably have consorted with 'navvies' (land navigators or canal builders who subsequently moved on to build the railways), 'coal whippers' and costermongers (today's barrow boys). Interestingly, Andy Serkis, the actor playing Bill Sikes, imagined that Sikes' father was a navvy: a strong, violent, hard-drinking thug who abandoned his infant son to a life of crime. That, in the context of the day, would have been eminently possible. As a toddler, Sikes could well have been taken into a lodging house that provided a front for professional child thieves. Some of those houses even ran schools for pickpockets in their kitchens. Independence, even for small children, was a highly valued commodity. And those children became adults very quickly. They had to: in the more desperate slums the average age of death was seventeen. But they had time enough to become parents – the age of consent was twelve.

Thus the sort of reckless abandon with which the likes of the Artful Dodger approached life makes some sense – more so in light of the fact that crime did pay, sometimes extremely well. A pickpocket in the 1830s could earn a much as six shillings a day, while a professional cabinetmaker earned less than that in a week. Yet Fagin's gang of thieves and pickpockets risked the most appalling punishments if they were caught. Assaults on people commonly resulted in a fine or a very short jail sentence, but theft, even of a few pounds worth of goods, usually led to transportation. Nancy's 'peaching' on the gang was, then, the most brutal betrayal. She was sentencing all of them to death or transportation. In that light, her murder by Bill Sikes is, if not exactly forgivable, at least understandable.

But what of Fagin? Dickens apparently modelled him on a well-known Jewish fence called Ikey Solomon. And one can draw parallels between Fagin and the earlier exploits of another infamous fence, one Jonathan Wild. He was famed and feared for his ability to lure people into his employ, turn them into hardened criminals and then blackmail them with the threat of exposure and the gallows. Here there are shades of the relationship between Fagin and his boys, and especially Sikes. Fagin's 'day job' as a clothes trader, and his prowess at magic, would also have been factually based. Ashekenazim Jews in the nineteenth century often peddled clothes, and kept company with other foreign itinerants. Bleasdale's Fagin adds another, equally believable dimension to the character. We first meet him in the company of wandering musicians and street players, many of whom would also have been Jewish. Dickens' London was teeming with such people: Italian puppeteers and organ grinders with monkeys were ubiquitous ('Punch and Judy', incidentally, is of Italian origin). In many ways the life of a wandering musician or circus player was an attractive existence. As the Victorian era edged in, England became increasingly dominated by the sound of factory bells calling workers to their daily toil. To be a street acrobat, a fire-eater, contortionist, magician or any other form of strolling exhibitionist was a much freer – if sometimes suspect – alternative. It was a way of life that would be gradually eroded in the second half of the century as communications grew with the coming of the railway age, and industrialisation increased to create a more cohesive society.

But Dickens was at pains to point out that, in *Oliver Twist*, there was nothing cohesive about society in the 1830s. Hence the three distinct worlds: that of the Workhouse, of Fagin, and (the one which he addressed least successfully) of Brownlow. Oliver may have thought that he 'belonged to the world again' when he woke up in Brownlow's well-appointed Pentonville town-house, but it wasn't the world that Dickens was concerned with. He was firmly entrenched in the sorry citadels where the 'surplus classes' lurked: a couple of miles and light years away from the drawing rooms of the tee-totalling Brownlows and Bedwins.

chapter 3

Location, Location, Location

On Set, Behind the Scenes, and (occasionally) Beyond the Pale

By her own admission, Sophia Myles (playing Oliver's mother Agnes) didn't really know what she was letting herself in for. She spent the best part of a day splattered with mud, harnessed to the cliff, pretending to be suicidal. By the end of the day, it was a case of illusion meeting reality; Sophia was not a happy bunny. The scene was shot at Old Harry Rocks near Studland in Dorset.

Recreating Dickens' World

The first seven scenes of Oliver Twist run like this:
Agnes on a cliff top; Agnes stumbling towards a seaside town; Agnes entering the town and subsequently the Workhouse; Agnes giving birth and dying.
Simple.
Here's how they were filmed. On day one, Sophia Myles, the actress playing the hapless Agnes, was hosed down, splattered with mud, harnessed to a cliff in Studland, Dorset and remained there on and off for the best part of a day while she was filmed from a helicopter. The latter part of the day was spent filming her stumbling towards the seaside town that we see in the distance. But there is no seaside town: special effects created it.

Two weeks later it *is* real: the crew moved to the town of Alston in Cumbria, several hundred miles to the north. The scenes of Agnes being carried to the Workhouse were also filmed there. But the scenes of her giving birth in that Workhouse were not. They were filmed six weeks later on a set in Barrandov Film Studios in Prague.

Complicated. And, later, surreal. Other interiors of the Workhouse were filmed in the disused grain silo of a Czech monastery. Some London and Rome interiors were filmed in other parts of the monastery; Marienbad stood in for the spas of Rome; Mr Brownlow's front door is in King's Bench Walk in London, but pass through it and you're in Barrandov studios again. Mrs Leeford's Paris apartment is in the best restaurant in Prague; Bill Sikes' front door is in a less salubrious part of Prague and Fagin's den, supposedly in the sensationally vile London slum of Jacob's Island, is actually in the medieval town of Chesky Krumlov, a site second only to Venice on UNESCO's world heritage list.

part 1

The word 'why' springs to mind. Why shoot a large part
of a quintessentially English drama in the Czech Republic?
And why scoot about all over England?

Back to simplicity for the answer. Nobody's denying that
the main reason is money: it's cheaper to film in the Czech
Republic. But Producer Keith Thompson adds that 'I'd seen
Barrandov studios years ago and was incredibly taken by the
standard of construction (for set-builds). And I'd remembered
Prague as a place that had locations that would be suitable
for the world of Sikes and Fagin. Admittedly it's now full
of Armani and crystal shops, but it's still got a side that just
doesn't exist in London any more.'

The bottom line, however, was the budget. As line producer
(effectively, one notch down from the producer) Alison Barnett
explains, 'One thing was obvious from the start: if we wanted
to film these scripts we were going to be in trouble if we tried to
do it all in the UK. Financially there was no way.' She goes on
to say that filming in the Czech Republic is about a third
cheaper than filming in the UK 'except filming in the streets of
Prague itself: that's much more expensive than London.'

The town of Alston in Cumbria.
It provided an extraordinary
number of locations: amongst
them the exteriors of the
Workhouse; the Funeral
Parlour, the cemetery and a
pub. Some scenes here had
to match up to interior scenes
shot in or near Prague, and
the main problem was always
windows. You won't find
a single sash window in the
Czech Republic.

This location, once 'dressed', was the view from the pub where Sally celebrates her theft of the locket in Episode One. It had to be recreated for a scene in Episode Four when Monks meets Bumble – and by that time the crew were in Prague. The recreation is actually a painted backdrop.

Anyone who has been to Prague will understand why film crews have flocked here to shoot period pieces including *Amadeus, Joan of Arc, Yentl, Les Miserables* and *The Scarlet Pimpernel*: Prague *is* a period piece. And although no-one is going to discuss budgets on the streets of that city or anywhere else, here's a tiny indication of the sort of costs involved: for something on the scale of *Oliver Twist*, petrol costs alone amount to around £ 6,000 a week.

No wonder people prefer Prague. But that leads to other problems – like scheduling and continuity. As Alison says, 'I worked out that we could only shoot in the UK for seven weeks and we would have to be in and around Prague for the other twelve. Then I do a basic schedule structure according to, for example, the availability of Barrandov Studios. Then, once the budget is approved, we can start crewing. And, to be honest, I can't wait for the 1st Ad (first assistant director) to come on board and fine-tune the schedule. It's a real weight off my mind.' The 1st Ad (in this case Peter Freeman) is responsible for the seemingly loopy notion of filming the first seven scenes over a period of seven weeks in several different locations. But he can't do that until they've actually found their locations...

'How long's a piece of string?' is Keith Thompson's response when asked how long it takes to find locations. 'It isn't a quantifiable thing. Sometimes you find them immediately and other times it takes forever. We had Czech and English location teams on the go at the same time. Our real find in the Czech Republic was Doksany (the monastery) and our major success in England was Alston. It was perfect for so many locations: the Workhouse exterior; the funeral parlour; the exterior of Sowerberry's shop; the cemetery; Oliver's solitary room...' Poor old Alston. Anyone would be forgiven for thinking it's perfectly hideous. The point is, it had the potential to be dressed down to look dismal.

You won't find sail makers or indeed boats in Alston – it's 2000 feet above sea-level. Many locals were hired as extras to populate the 'seaside' town.

Construction designer Malcolm Thornton is the man largely responsible for making blameless buildings look hideous, dismal and decrepit – or exotic, palatial or provincial. He and art director Stevie Herbert design the overall 'look' of the inanimate parts of *Oliver Twist* – and that means everything from Fagin's den to a pot lid. 'For a TV production,' says Malcolm, 'this is a huge project. We've got an enormous amount of sets to build (in the Barrandov Studios) and then, with the locations, one of the biggest problems is finding a consistent vision of Prague for England and England for Prague. We've had to find Czech places that could pass for England without having to spend a lot of a limited budget actually making them look English. That's partly why we decided not to go down the architectural route. I'm not, anyway, interested in going where others have gone before, and I don't want this to be a history lesson. It's the visual impact of places that I'm keen on – interesting shapes for the camera to find. And knowing that we were going to have to use Prague drove us to find English locations that weren't as literal as you might expect.'

Ditto the Czech Republic. As Stevie says, 'It's really rather sad. There are all these stunning buildings and we're going 'yes, yes, it's beautiful, but show us the nasty crumbling bits. We want the horrid dark corners.' Stevie, in fact, is an expert in horrid corners. Overseeing the set builds at Barrandov, she is forever inspecting how the workmen have interpreted her drawings of crumbling plaster and sad rooms, and added paint stains and pigeon droppings. 'The upside is that I get to meet a lot of men,' she says with a laugh, 'but all we talk about is mouldings…'

It's detail like mouldings, cornices, windows and door hinges that really matter when you're trying to match two entirely disparate styles of architecture. You won't find a sash window in the Czech Republic, so they have to be built from scratch – an operation that poses its own problems. 'The standard of workmanship here is incredibly high,' says Malcolm, 'but, understandably, the craftsmen have no idea what egg-and-dart cornicing or sash windows look like so they're having to ask us for details about everything. You can't use the shorthand you're accustomed to in England.' Another major difference is colour: buildings in the Czech Republic, apart from being finished with a plaster render, are generally painted in shades of ochre. A close inspection of the exterior of Newgate Prison (one of the very last shots in the series) reveals it to be coated with very un-English yellowy plaster. It's actually that Czech grain silo again.

Julie Walters (Mrs Mann) and David Ross (Mr Bumble) look out from in the former's sitting room in the workhouse. It's a good example of split locations:
the exterior of the room is in Alston – the interior is in a monastery bang on the main road from Prague to Dresden.

Although the conundrum of what to film in the Czech Republic and what to film in England was largely solved before locations had been found, there were a few unexpected hiccups. The market scene where we first glimpse Fagin in Episode one, for instance, was scheduled to be filmed at the Rotunda outside Bart's Hospital in Smithfield. 'It's a Victorian loading bay,' explains Malcolm, 'and we chose it because as it goes deeper and deeper into the ground towards the bottom of the ramp you go from formal Georgian architecture to Fagin's world of crumbling plaster – which ties in to some of the exteriors of Prague. Unfortunately we lost this location and had to relocate the scene in Prague, but the concept held good of not using classic London architecture.' Just as well, really, because the replacement was a Czech town called Kolin. 'We used the side of a Gothic church with flying buttresses for the market scene,' he finished. 'And it's got grey stone buildings round it. Not really London and not typically Czech either.'

At one stage the Jacob's Island scenes (Fagin's new den where Bill Sikes falls to his death) were scheduled to be filmed in England as well. Location Manager Jane Soames found an old Victorian ice factory in Grimsby. 'It was really interesting – too late in period but that didn't bother me,' says Malcolm. 'It had gantrys and walkways, it was crumbling to bits and had lots of timbers holding it up.' In stunning contrast to Grimsby ice factories, they ended up in the fabulous town of Chesky Krumlov.

Another location (again lost very late in the day) was London's Trinity Church Square. 'That,' says Malcolm, 'was going to be the exterior of Brownlow's house. We always knew the interior was going to be at Barrandov because we needed the space, but the problem in this case was that the interior was already under construction at Barrandov when we lost the exterior. Jane was therefore committed to find a building to match it: it *had* to be Georgian and have three windows on the right of the front door.' She did find somewhere – King's Bench Walk in Inner Temple – but it didn't work from every angle. 'We had almost 360 degree shooting in Trinity Church Square,' recalls Malcolm, 'and the replacement had only about 180 degrees' (i.e., film at a wider angle and you'll include Tescos or something equally un-Georgian). 'We had about five or six days for me to design to the other side of the street and for it to be built. It's actually quite exceptional to have to build fifty metres of street.' Keith Thompson, on the other hand, remembers something exceptionally difficult about the shoot at King's Bench Walk: 'Trying to clear the area of Porsches and BMWs. Nightmare.'

Using split locations is actually a perfectly normal filming procedure. It's very common to arrive at a front door in one country and, tardis-like, walk through into a different country several weeks later. Beaming down to Barrandov, one finds that Emily Woof, playing Nancy, has done exactly that. On day four of shooting, she arrived at Brownlow's house in London the pouring rain (well, under a rain machine), fainted, and was carried inside by Dr Losberne. Forty-two days later, she's playing the next scene in the drawing room – otherwise known as Stage 4 at Barrandov. (Spare a thought for her: she's had a six-week gap in between these two scenes, and the one she's playing now is her most important. And it's one of the longest in the entire drama, running to nearly five pages.)

'Trying to clear the area of Porsches and BMWs. Nightmare.'

left and above: King's Bench Walk in London. Normally populated by barristers and BMWs, it's been dressed for a more sedate century. All the exteriors of Brownlow's house were shot here.

41

above: Rehearsing the scene in which the truth about Oliver's parentage is revealed. Michael Kitchen (Brownlow) is showing him the locket with the miniatures of his parents and his mother's lock of hair. The scene is a long and a vital one – five pages of script – and took more than a day to film.

Note the net curtains: they serve the purpose of disguising the fact that the room is a set-build, inside the studio at Barrandov.

right: There's no skimping as regards the props. Every piece of furniture and every ornament is the genuine article: antique and imported from England.

The drawing room is a perfect reproduction of an elegant, monied Georgian interior – apart from the fact that it doesn't have a ceiling. Or that the pillars are actually plastic. As Malcolm Thornton says, 'if you get all the vital details right, people aren't going to even think about the fact that something may be fake.' And the pillars are the only things that are fake. Everything else, from teacups to writing-desks, carpets to paintings are antiques imported from England. Barrandov, the second largest studio complex in continental Europe, has an impressive array of items for hire (including 10, 000 pieces of furniture and 65, 000 prop pieces), but they have a dearth of Georgian furniture. Hence the imported English artefacts.

More antiques can be found in Brownlow's study, in the hallway, in Rose's upstairs bedroom (which isn't upstairs at all) and in the half-landing outside her room. Half-landing, in this case, means literally half of a landing – not a landing half-way up the stairs. You only design as much of a set as is going to be seen on TV.

Inside the drawing room, however, the actors are rehearsing under the direction of Renny Rye – and a girl with a rapt expression is standing behind Renny. This is something she, Sam Donovan, does a lot – in fact she never leaves Renny's side. She was there on day one and she'll still be there nineteen weeks later. It's got nothing to do with a peculiar fascination for Renny, but with her job as script supervisor – better known as continuity girl. (For some funny reason, they're always girls. And although there *is* a rogue male in that arm of the industry, he's *still* known as a continuity girl.)

A spruced-up Oliver. The candles in the background can pose a potential nightmare as regards continuity. Scenes where they're lit may be shot several times – sometimes days apart – but the candles have to burn in 'screen time'.

The continuity girl is the vital link between split locations, and much else besides. The title may have a distinct whiff of the holiday camp about it – but Sam's job is no holiday. She has to keep a record of everything that happens during shooting. And that means *everything*. She'll note how long each scene takes to film, how many takes have been shot and why some can be used and others not; she'll record the details of the camera and lenses being used, the position of the actors, whether or not furniture has been moved, how far candles have burned down and whether or not they're overrunning. If you want to know anything about anything – ask Sam. And if, God forbid, the laboratory ruins a film then, thanks to her, they can film it again days, or even weeks, later in exactly the same way.

But now, as Emily Woof prepares for her vital scene, Sam is explaining another aspect of her job. 'When Nancy arrived at the house she was soaking wet. It's now six weeks later, but continuity-wise it's probably about five minutes. This scene starts with Nancy already in the drawing room, so we can assume that she's a little drier than she was and we've got a little leeway. Wardrobe have sprayed her a bit, but what I've got to remember is that *Losberne* also has to be slightly damp. He carried the dripping Nancy into the house, so he'll be a bit wet round the middle and chest.'

That sort of problem – although a major link – is common to any drama, but costume dramas carry another potential continuity problem in the shape of candles. 'I plot roughly how long (in screen time) each scene takes,' says Sam, 'and then keep an eye on the candles to see that they correspond. But it can be problematic. The candles are lit for rehearsals [for the benefit of the camera crew] and a scene might run to eight or nine takes. Obviously the candles are burning all the time and will be much lower in take nine than in take one. I take polaroids at the end of each take, but if an editor decides to use a little bit of take one and then a little bit of take nine then there's nothing I can do about it. I know I can do everything right at the time but there's nothing I can do about that. I'm history by then,' she adds with a relieved grin, 'I'm long gone.'

Seemingly small concerns, but they're vital for preventing anachronisms and anomalies. Anyone remember the film where Rudolph Valentino, in the middle of ancient Arabia, wore a Rolex? That was the fault of the costume department, but it wouldn't have escaped Sam's eagle eye. As she says 'my job crosses over into virtually every department: costume, lighting, editing, make-up, props...and the actors themselves. They'll often come up and say "Oh God, I've forgotten where I was sitting", or "How long am I supposed to have known the person I'm talking to?" If I've been doing my job properly I'll be able to tell them.'

And she *has* done her job properly. There are no continuity problems in Nancy's big scene.

Production Designer Malcolm Thornton in the studio at Barrandov with some of his models. They're actually miniatures of the building going on in the background: the stairs on the left of the picture, for example, are those leading to Fagin's den, and the bits of wood behind Malcolm will soon become The Three Cripples bar.

The art department is the largest in this production; there are up to 40 craftsmen working at any one time on building and dressing the sets. Most of them are Czech, and they have extraordinarily high standards. And they could teach the Brits a thing or two about recycling: they re-use everything, including the hessian that they use as a 'lining' for walls. Whether or not it has wallpaper or even plaster on top, it's painstakingly salvaged by a Barrandov employee after the set has been dismantled.

By now everyone is getting rather bored with being in Brownlow's house. They've been filming there for ten days now ('wretched man never goes out' laughs his *alter ego* Michael Kitchen), and they're about to move onto the next location – Stage 6 at Barrandov, the setting for many of Stevie Herbert's nasty little corners and sad pieces of wood.

It was also, in the past, the setting for something really *very* nasty. In the 1930s, Goebbles' Nazi propaganda films were shot here; the vast 2000 square-metre stage echoing to the sound of goose-stepping and rallying cries to the Führer. Ironic, then, that the studios were founded (in 1931) by one Vaclav Havel, uncle of the present Czech president and noted opponent of totalitarianism.

Despite its age, Barrandov has kept pace with the British and American film industries as regards facilities, but it's a great brooding barrack of a place with nothing to recommend it in the design department. The last interior designers to visit, one suspects, were graduates of the Communist school of 'magnolia-goes-with-everything'. And here, off the mile-long corridors behind Stage 6, are the production offices of *Oliver Twist*. If one really wants to know what goes on behind the scenes, look no further.

The Living Doll

'I'm trying to locate the baby!' shouts an anguished Alison Barnett. 'We know it's left Shepperton but it seems to have gone astray. And we can't reschedule it – it's needed back there for *Gormenghast...*'

Her cries interrupt production co-ordinator Sara Hamill and assistant accountant Nicky Coates who are talking about schedules for cars to Doksany, a possible camera replacement and (rather more vitally) the best place to buy underwear in Teddington. More to the point, they seem to know what Alison's talking about and Sara reacts accordingly. She gets on the phone to London and, ten minutes later, locates the missing baby. For those totally flummoxed by what's going on (this writer included), light is shed on the situation by discovering that the missing baby is an animatronic – sort of upmarket living doll-version of Oliver. He is due to be born the following day and is on loan from Shepperton where he's being used in the BBC's adaptation of Mervyn Peake's *Gormenghast* trilogy.

Alison goes back to her cost reports, but there are other teething troubles with the baby. It appears it has broken its leg in transit, and a further phone conversation ensues about where to mend it: London or Prague? Prague seems to fit the bill as it's vital that the baby (later christened Charlie) is born on schedule. The props department are confident that they can mend the leg, and make-up comes to the rescue as regards the missing umbilical chord. Lesley Lamont-Fisher says she will construct it out of a condom filled with purple-dyed gelatine and wrapped with cotton thread. (If all this seems bizarre just wait for the arrival of Uncle Richard's goitre.)

The job of production co-ordinator is probably best described as the off-set equivalent of what Sam Donovan does on-set. If Sam is concerned that the filming is fluid, Sara ensures that everything else runs like clockwork. The only way to really get a grip on what she does is by eavesdropping.

'Don't laugh or I'll thump you,' she says to Lukas the runner, after the baby question has been addressed. With that, she hands him the next day's call-sheet (basically, a schedule of what's being filmed, who will be on set, who will be picked up at what time by what driver, when lunch will be available and for how many and what requirements have been listed from every department; and the weather forecast.) Lukas *does* laugh: he's correcting her Czech translations and some of them make for interesting reading. But Sara doesn't thump him. She's too busy (and, it has to be said, too nice), and is now tackling a problem that has something to do with A-frames. Then she moves onto laundry for the cast and crew. Next someone pokes their head round the office door and asks her to order a car. Two minutes later is transpires that there's been a potential disaster in the development lab and would Sara – because she knows a little bit about everything – fly to London with the negative to see
if it can be rescued? Sara duly flies to London, but not before reminding Lukas that 'I need a translation for morning cakes. Morning refreshments are causing consternation on set.' Then she's off, leaving assistant co-ordinator Tim Gorman in charge. Like Sara, Tim is endlessly flexible and good-humoured. You really have to be if you're a co-ordinator.

The Birth of Oliver

Despite a last-minute panic when he was detained at customs, Charlie has arrived safely. Equipped with a mended leg and that umbilical cord, he's now in the process of being born. Not once, not twice, but several times. His mother, whose labour pains started in Dorset, continued in Cumbria and are now nearing completion in Prague, is lying on a table ('I wasn't allowed a bed. I'm not sure if it was because Marc Warren and I had already broken three...') is stoically enduring her multiple births. The doctor, in the shape of Michael Bertenshaw, is doing likewise. 'Well, I can't afford to make a mess of it, can I? There would be no story of he was still-born.' Liz Smith, playing the dipsomanaical Sally, is being roasted by the fire. Renny Rye is aware that she's hotter than she may have expected, but there's nothing he can do about it. They don't mess about when constructing hearths in the Czech Republic: they make the real thing, brick surrounds, proper flues and all. In England, it would be an 'effect' fire. Here it's the real McCoy although, being gas, it can at least be extinguished between takes. Charlie the animatronic baby looks like the real McCoy as well: the only problem is that he can't cry.

That's why there are some stand-by babies – real ones. The new-born Olivers were recruited from a Prague orphanage and, as Alison Barnett was reliably informed, are the offspring of gypsy women who come to Prague to give birth...and then leave. Everyone is rather subdued about them. But, when the first baby arrives, he seems to adore being coated in gel by Lesley Lamont-Fisher and really doesn't seem to mind being born again. Nor does the second Oliver, nor the third who, strictly speaking, is an Olivia.

This scene has two separate versions as it's actually two scenes: one at the beginning and one at the end of Episode one. And it contains all the vital elements around which the plot of *Oliver Twist* revolves. The props requirements for the day read 'Doctor's bag, Sally's gin bottle, sixpence, Leeford's locket and chain with miniature, Leeford's ring with inscription, patchwork coverlet, dummy baby'. But that's not the only reason why the filming takes so long – there are strict regulations about using babies (hence a morning, noon and an afternoon baby). Furthermore, you can hardly instil acting skills into a new-born. But after it's all over, Renny Rye is delighted. 'I'm pretty sure we'll use one of the real babies. He held his fists out in the air as Michael swung him round: very real-life...very fight-for-life...very Oliver.'

The Baby Farm

'Finding a Baby Farm,' says Keith Thompson, 'was one of the most difficult things. 'For a start, who knows what a baby farm is supposed to look like? It's not as if there are a lot of them around...'

Regardless of aesthetics, the main criterion was that it had to be in the English countryside. The exterior shots here are important: we see Oliver being brought to the farm on a bright summer's day in June 1826, and then collected nine years later on a snowy day. It's all got to look frightfully Gainsborough – even if it's slap in the middle of the Czech Republic. 'Perhaps you oughtn't to look *too* closely at the architecture,' muses Keith – risking a smack round the head from Malcolm Thornton. 'I spent a *fortune* on this place,' Malcolm says. 'It was a complete wreck when we found it. Most of the money went on safety: I get a bit peeved when I have to spend my budget on things you can't see...' Then he looks closely at the things you *can* see. 'I think it looks a bit like a 1960s Essex house. All you need is a couple of Doric columns...'

Joking apart, the search for the Baby Farm was the prickliest thorn in the flesh of *Oliver*. They found a perfect location in the UK that required no money to be spent on it – but the schedule couldn't handle a UK shoot. It *had* to be filmed in the Czech Republic. Lala the Czech location manager (not his real name but even his Czech colleagues can't remember what that is) had even less of a clue what a Baby Farm was supposed to look like, and time was running short. 'We were on the very last recce,' recalls Malcolm, 'and we were supposed to be flying back to England within a few hours. Lala said he'd seen this place that might do so we went there – but couldn't get to it. The road was flooded and we tried to hire a boat to get to it by river but there weren't any. It was a nightmare.' But they arrived eventually, had time for a quick look, went back to England and wrote 'Baby Farm, Vbrno, Czech Republic' into the schedule.

opposite: 1960s Essex Man, typically Dickensian or terribly un-English? Opinion was divided as to whether or not the Baby Farm looked like the real McCoy. It was a difficult location to find, not least because nobody really knows what baby farms did look like. In the main, they were in rural areas, and there's no doubt that this is countrified. But they don't do ivy in the Czech Republic, so the creeping green stuff is fake.

So, shown **above**, is the snow. The scenes shot here (depositing and then collecting Oliver) spanned a decade but had to be shot in one day. The temperature on that day was nearly 100 degrees – hell for chancing snowflakes.

And now here they are, filming the arrival of the baby Oliver. The set-up probably *would* have fooled Gainsborough. You wouldn't have wanted him to spend too long looking at the ivy on the building itself (it's fake), but the lush grass is real and so are the remarkably English-looking trees. But one only has a few hours to appreciate them: after lunch they cut the grass, trimmed some of the trees, put foam on the ground, wheeled in the snow machine...and ushered in a winter's day nine years later. It's not only the landscape that looks different. Suddenly David Ross (Mr Bumble) comes trundling out of his trailer, many pounds heavier than he was before lunch, which has nothing to do with what he ate. 'I've just had a clothes change, age change, wig change, weight change and teeth change,' he announces with glee. Then he barrels off to the Baby Farm to collect a small blonde boy and propel him into the further adventures of *Oliver Twist*.

A few hours later the crew leave Vbrno. It's Saturday night and, as usual, they've been working fourteen hours a day, six days a week. They're exhausted – Sunday is their only day off. Many of them will spend that day in quiet contemplation. There are no prizes for guessing why: after Saturday night, some can't even contemplate moving.

Doksany

'Keeping up morale is part of my job,' says Renny Rye. 'People are working all day, six days a week – it's hard. Also we're working split days at the moment and people tend not to like them very much.' Split days *are* pretty vile: they're the filmic version of changing time zones: when day shoots move towards night shoots and the cast and crew find themselves starting work at midday and finishing at or after midnight. Everyone agrees that although the working hours are the same, any spare time is somehow lost. It becomes a case of falling into bed at one or two in the morning, getting up and going to work, and then repeating the process. Not popular.

But that lack of popularity doesn't reflect on the man responsible for breaking-down the schedule. He's Peter Freeman, the 1st AD; the man who basically had to fill in the blanks of Alison Barnett's rough schedule of 'three weeks here' and 'six weeks there'. It sounds gruesomely complicated but Peter insists that while it might not be everyone's cup of tea, 'it's quite a fun process. It's exactly like a jigsaw or a logic puzzle.' In a nutshell, he has to juggle with the 422 scenes of *Oliver Twist*, several locations, hundreds of people, travel times, actors' availability, the scripts themselves – and then come up with a formula that translates into a workable shooting schedule. 'And,' says Peter, 'you have to take into account the amount of time it takes for things like putting lamps and camera equipment into trucks and moving them to a different location.' And this is his idea of fun? Peter grins and tucks into his breakfast of sausage and scrambled eggs (it's 1pm but that's his fault – he scheduled breakfast as well). 'Complicated fun.

It usually takes about four or five hours to break down a one-hour script – and then you go back and do it again. And again. I come on the recce to all the locations and usually find myself back at the hotel room sticking little post-its notes on the mirror and then moving them all around thinking "We're here, so we can film that scene from Episode One here, move that scene from Episode Five there"...and then I have to start all over again. You have to whittle everything down again and again – there's always one little scene that gets left behind so you have to go back and find a place for it.' The bottom line is that Peter has to make sure that filming can run fluidly for every hour and every day of this nineteen-week shoot. 'Period drama always takes slightly longer – usually about three weeks per hour.' But this series is seven hours long: that makes 21 weeks. 'So it does,' muses Peter. 'Now you know why everyone says it's a tight schedule...'

So it's probably just as well they found somewhere like Doksany, where they were able to base fourteen locations. A former monastery established in the twelfth century, parts of it are currently under restoration: other parts reveal the place to be a hotch-potch of hugely differing architectural styles. The guidebook has it that 'words do not suffice to describe all the beautiful highlights of Doksany' (which lets this writer off the hook) but which isn't actually true. The place isn't particularly beautiful: its appeal lies more in its romantic decrepitude – with the glaring exception of the stunning baroque Church of the Birth of Our Lady. Mrs Mann and Mr Bumble get married here, in the crypt.

part 2

The monastery of Doksany. It provided a host of
locations for the production. The wing seen above
contains the Scottish lawyer's office in Rome,
Mrs Leeford's London apartment, the staircase
entrance to her Paris apartment and Mr Grimwig's
London office. What is really strange about the
wing is that it appears uniform from the outside but,
internally, contains varying styles of architecture.
As ever with locations in the Czech Republic, the art
department had to disguise both the windows and
the view – they built louvred shutters for each of the
rooms mentioned above.

left: the workhouse dining room where Oliver famously asks for more. It's in the basement at Doksany and was riddled with dust. Most of the crew wore face masks to film here. The cast, being on the other end of the camera, weren't so fortunate.

right: Mrs Mann's sitting-room with the portraits of her late and not terribly lamented husband. He's actually none other than producer Keith Thompson, making a fly-on-the wall appearance in his production.

'I've never been anywhere as useful as Doksany,' says Malcolm Thornton. As he speaks, he's climbing a staircase currently being kitted-out as the entrance hall of Mrs Leeford's Paris apartment. It leads, however, into an enfilade of rooms starting with Mr Leeford's Rome drawing room and anteroom (which, seen from a different angle, is Mr Grimwig's London office), leading into an enormous frescoed refectory which becomes the Scottish lawyer's office in Rome. That, in turn, leads to Mrs Leeford's London drawing room and bedroom – into which Mr Grimwig disappears because half of it is actually his clerk's room.

One could go on. The point, really, is how does Malcolm decide which room is which? He talks of finding 'Mrs Leeford's room' as if, Miss Havisham-like, she's been there all along. Well she hasn't. There's *nothing* there. It's just a large, empty room with some rather dingy wallpaper. 'Quite,' says Malcolm. 'It's rather eerie, isn't it? And a bit frayed round the edges. Exactly like Mrs Leeford in decline.'

This is a politically correct book. It contains two no smoking signs.

Then you look at the wallpaper and realise it could quite easily pass for being English – but there's no way that giant Northern European porcelain heater thing in the corner could claim to live in London. 'No. We're covering it with a giant firescreen which has English fabric on one side and Italian on the other. There's another stove like that in Mr Leeford's Rome apartment, so we're using the same firescreen back to front.' You look again at the room chosen for that apartment and begin to see why Malcolm ear-marked it for Italy. The ceiling is higher; the room is lighter and there's no wallpaper. And so on...It's all about knowing what you're doing, having years of experience – and getting those skilled Czech craftsmen to make louvered shutters for all the windows to hide the fact that they look on to the parkland surrounding Doksany, and not the streets of Rome or London.

Cut to Mrs Mann's apartment in the Workhouse – across the courtyard at Doksany. Most of the Workhouse interiors are in some part or other of the monastery complex, but Mrs Mann's apartment is right next to the main road to Dresden. Thundering juggernauts have no place in Dickens, so the police are on hand to stop the traffic when the cameras roll. And they're almost there, ready to capture the scene of Mrs Mann mourning the passing of the husband she hasn't seen for fourteen years. There are portraits of him all over her walls – and he looks vaguely familiar. It's Keith Thompson. 'I always try to make a Hitchcock-type appearance in my films,' he grins, 'but my acting's obviously so bad they've reduced me to a fly on the wall.'

the workhouse boardroom

The Workhouse Boardroom. The board members are played by (left to right): David Foxxe, Ken Parry, Desmond Barritt, Richard Sims and Hugh Lloyd.

Then the traffic is stopped, the cameras roll, Mr Bumble makes his pass at the mourning Mrs Mann – and they're interrupted by the screams of baby Oliver. It's another baby day, but a slightly less fraught one. Today's Olivers (again there are three) are slightly older. The only problem is they all have different coloured hair. Continuity is provided by the creative use of a bonnet.

Elsewhere at Doksany, Malcolm Thornton is inspecting the work being done in the Workhouse Boardroom, the dining room, the women's dormitory, and the 'sad apartment'. This last location is the ghastly hovel (the exterior was filmed in Alston) where Oliver is taken when he is apprenticed to Sowerberry the undertaker. It was referred to as a 'sad apartment' in the script – so that's what everyone calls it: ditto a 'dirty derelict room' and Mrs Leeford's 'genteel apartment'. You get used to people rushing around saying 'how's the sad apartment getting on?' Malcolm, now walking towards the mill where the Bumbles sell the locket to Monks, has had to get used to more of his budget disappearing on safety measures. 'We have freelance safety people coming out from England, and we have to do what they say. We had to re-floor the mill, for example. I do get a little miffed when people can't actually *see* what I've spent my money on...'

But then again, you can't have Julie Walters plummeting to her death through dodgy floorboards. Very expensive.

Barrandov

Studio 6 at Barrandov with ten set-builds under construction. It's in this 2,000 square metre space that Nazi propaganda films were shot in the late 1930s. Since then more than 2,500 films have been made in the 12 stages that contsitute the complex. Local and foreign productions can make use of a quarter of a million costume items, 20,000 pairs of shoes, 10,000 pieces of furniture, 9,000 wigs, 22,000 carpets, 65,000 pieces of props as well as saddles, carriages and weapons.

Stevie Herbert is 'terrifically excited' about the set-build on Barrandov Studios' Stage 6. 'Although,' she adds, only half-joking, 'that will change to resentment when the crew move in. And there's no way I'm going to be anywhere near the place when they strike (dismantle) the sets.' This may all sound a little extreme, but if you consider that Stevie has spent months on hundreds of scale drawings and on seeing those creations gradually come to life, one can understand her point of view.

Those creations are breathtaking and, in the world of television, highly unusual. It's rare to build so many studio sets – even more exceptional to build them to such a high standard. The latter is entirely due to the quality of the Czech craftsmen and materials. Where in England scaffolding would be used, here they have weathered timber from their own yard. And that's a massive bonus: it means that the timbers one sees on screen – in for, example, The Three Cripples tavern – need no 'dressing down' or weathering. They're just hauled in from the backyard. And the solidity of the sets is remarkable – a source of comfort to the actors and a benefit for the sound department.

There are ten set-builds in the enormous expanse of Stage 6, of which Fagin's den is the largest. And one of the most important. It's a major departure from the loft-like versions of the den which previous adaptations, and indeed Dickens, had offered. 'Historically,' says Malcolm, 'I discovered that the areas of Spittalfields and Saffron Hill in East London were once populated by merchants who moved out as they became more rich and successful. Their houses were then taken over by vagrants and scallywags...and they became the Rookeries of Dickens' day. The idea that these houses were once half-decent made me think that we should set the den in one of them rather rather than the more traditional roof loft space that we've seen before.'

The den he finally designed is actually composed of two houses. 'You go up an alley through an open courtyard which is one house – a Huguenot weaver's house with a loft as described in the book – but, but halfway up the stairs they've broken through the wall into the room of another, grander house adjacent to that courtyard.' As he speaks he climbs the stair (he does that a lot) and stops at the hole in the wall. It's all very odd for someone who doesn't have the complete – and completed – picture in their head. Yes, one can imagine this as Fagin's den, but the reality is that the alley below doesn't exist – it's miles away in the gypsy town of Zatec. ('Props to include drinks, newspaper, Pedlar's suitcase, practical flaming Braziers, goody bags...bottle of gin.') And it's difficult to hear what Malcolm's saying because there are workmen in the background building, amongst other things, Sowerberry's kitchen cellar, Fagin's prison cell and The Three Cripples tavern. Still, reality and illusion and all that...and the ideas that Malcolm has come up with are nothing less than stunning.

The den is in the grander house. 'It's an early Georgian interior, but the doors have been ripped off, and the gang have utilised what's left and put it to their own uses. The table you see them sitting at is an old Georgian door rather than old planks, and in the corner there's a cobwebbed Georgian chandelier. And,' says Malcolm with relish, 'the plaster is crumbling and it's all _so_ dirty.'

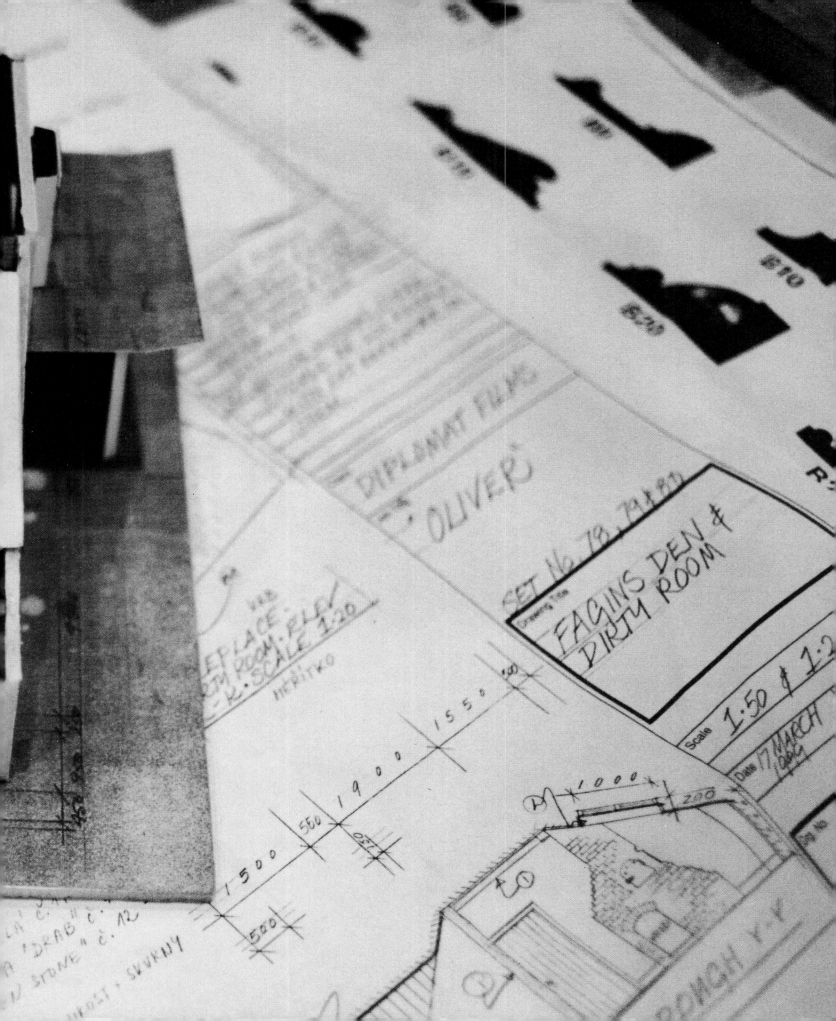

Dirt is important to this production. Given the stupefying nastiness of the living conditions of the poor and the 'underclasses' of the day, everyone felt it was vital to get as close to reality as possible. Renny Rye later says that 'I want it to feel dirty – and it does. If you look at Doksany, some of the cast and crew are going around with face masks on, we're living through dirt half the time. And for anything to look dirty on screen it has to be twice as dirty in reality.'

Fagin's den, although not yet 'dressed' – a rather incongruous way of saying riddled with filth – is coming along nicely. 'Historically,' continues Malcolm, 'it's placed reasonably accurately. And it gives us the opportunity to add more than a loft space would. That's one of major changes we've imposed on book...combining this courtyard exterior with this old house. And because Fagin's den is now nine feet in the air it lets us shoot from different angles. The design process can offer opportunities not just for the look of the film but for the action as well. When they escape we can utilise the holes we've made in the floors, and the pigeons Fagin produces from his coat can go through holes in the ceiling into the roof beams. The sets can interact with the characters themselves.'

Of the other nine sets sharing Studio 6 with Fagin's den, Sowerberry's funeral parlour is one with the most complicated match to a split location. They filmed the approach to the parlour in Alston, and, while they're only filming interiors in Barrandov, the parlour has a window through which you can see Alston. Except it isn't Alston. It's a giant painted backdrop and a bit of pavement. A sad bit of pavement.

above: the exterior of Fagin's den.

left: the bottom two pictures show Fagin's den in various stages of construction in Studio 6, and the set builders in the top photograph are recreating Newgate Prison.

The Goitre of Marienbad

Uncle Richard's goitre is developing a life of its own. It's due to fly out shortly and there's something of a debate in the production office about whether or not it should go unaccompanied. The debate doesn't last long. For a start, what would Czech Customs make of a goitre? Even more important, it has to be attached to Uncle Richard in the spa at Marienbad and, as Alison Barnett says, 'we don't want it floating off on into the water...'

Goitres – huge growths from an enlarged thyroid – don't really happen any more. They resulted from an iodine imbalance: something that can easily be corrected nowadays. So the only goitres you'll see are ones like Uncle Richard's, made at considerable expense by a firm called Animated Extras. Which really does imply that it has a life of its own.

Amber Sibley, the make-up artist responsible for this grisly creation, will now fly out and take control of it. Apart from the danger of it floating off on it's own, it has to be strong enough to carry Richard Leeford's weight as his nephew pulls him out of the water with it. Yuk.

A week later, Uncle Richard passes away according to plan. The goitre, however, is destined for a big brighter future. It has its own agent (this is true) and flies back to London for another job. Amber, its minder, is at its side.

Uncle Richard and his notorious goitre. He dies, but the goitre lived on...

The extras hired for the scenes shot in the spa were, in the event, deemed to be not quite fat enough. Lucy, the 3rd A.D., successfully recruited several vast German tourists instead.

Chesky Krumlov

The castle at Chesky Krumlov is one of the most astonishing sights in Central Europe. Forty buildings and five courtyards were built over the course of six centuries as various noble families – Rosembergs, Eggenbergs and Schwarzenbergs – took control of this strategic area of Southern Bohemia. Endless parades of magnificent rooms, as well as the most important and perfectly preserved Baroque theatre on this planet, bear testament to the grandeur (and self-aggrandisement) of these families. These were people who had everything, and they didn't shy away from ostentation.

They did, however, remain a little coy about the possibility of having to make a quick getaway from revolting peasants. Closed to the public, and largely unknown, are the interconnecting attics and corridors built to facilitate the evacuation of the aristocrats in the event of an insurrection. They've actually never been used as an escape route – until *Oliver Twist* came to Krumlov. At the end of Episode Five, when Fagin and Bill Sikes are escaping from the braying mob – and when Fagin kicks Bullseye to his death – they're not running through the rafters of some dismal slum, but of the spectacular Castle of Chesky Krumlov. The design team have excelled themselves as regards this castle: they've managed to find a selection of nasty dark corners in one of the most magnificent buildings in the Czech Republic.

Serendipity gave them that location. Malcolm Thornton recalls that they had all but given up hope of finding anywhere to film in Chesky Krumlov when, walking through a courtyard in the town, they ran into a Czech architectural historian who specialised (as you do) in rafters. Not only that, but he was fluent in English, took them into the attics around the courtyard (which used to be a nunnery), and then told them about the vast roof spaces of the nearby castle. The upshot of that happy meeting was that the attics of the Old Nunnery were perfect for Fagin's new den – 'we didn't have to do anything beyond hang a few rags on the rafters,' says Malcolm with glee. 'The place was horrible – covered in dust and absolutely *filthy*.' Ditto the castle attics, which, as far as the viewer is concerned, lead on from the den for the escape sequence. It's from here that Fagin and Bill leap out of a window to the third location used in Chesky Krumlov – an old mill back in the town. It's a shame, in a way, that they didn't actually leap out of one of the castle windows. They would, of course, have died and spoiled the plot – but they would have been reviving the ancient Czech tradition of defenestration. At critical points in the country's history, this bizarre form of political assassination – hurling people out of a window – invariably came into play. The Thirty Years' War that devastated half of Europe was, in fact, sparked in 1618 by Protestant noblemen throwing a clutch of Catholics out of a window of Prague Castle.

But that doesn't really have anything to do with *Oliver Twist*.

part 3

The scene at the old mill where Bill meets his death is one of the most complex and, according to Sam Smith, the 'coolest' in the entire production. On screen, one sees Fagin and Bill scrambling down a wooden staircase and running along a rickety walkway with the mob braying for their blood below. On location it was rather a different picture: a set that cost £20,000 and took six days to build, 98-degree heat, an action sequence that takes twelve hours to film and that will last one minute on air. And a parade of tourists wandering about in their swimming costumes, hauling canoes out of Bill Sikes' watery grave. All completely barking mad as far as the real world is concerned: perfectly normal in the strange celluloid sphere of television.

This is a vital scene: it ties in with the other parts of the chase, it culminates in Bill's death, it involves fifty Czech extras and requires stunt doubles for both Fagin and Bill. And stunts have to be co-ordinated with minute precision: the position of Bill's hand on the ledge has to match that of the double when, hours later, his fatal fall is filmed. That fall is filmed in two stages and, inevitably, more than once – which means that the bits of breaking wood have to be put together again. It's hugely complicated and involves seventeen camera set-ups (i.e., moving the cameras – there are three today – sixteen times in order to capture different angles of Fagin, Bill, the fall and the mob).

The colossal Castle of Chesky Krumlov. Don't even think about visiting the Czech Republic without coming here: there's a glittering Renaissance palace within these austere walls; there are triumphs of the arts of stucco and *trompe l'oeuil*, parades of magnificent rooms spanning nearly six centuries; a spectacular five-tiered bridge and a baroque theatre that, uniquely on this earth, contains the original auditorium, stage scenery, lighting, and 540 items of costumes and accessories. Intriguingly, there are also fifty 300-year-old special effects instruments: amongst them a rotating drum in which sand was poured into a metal lining to imitate the sound of rain. So think again if you ever considered that special effects was a modern phenomenon.

Even the most down-to-earth of actors on *Oliver Twist* were lost for words when they saw the theatre. Not that they had much time to appreciate it: they were bundled into the interconnecting castle attics – aka a putrid London slum – to enact the flight from Fagin's den.

It's not surprising there are a few hitches, some of them totally unexpected: Fagin's teeth go missing and are located at the lunch table; poor old Craster Pringle, who flew in to play a passing policeman, is ferried out to hospital after a chair snaps and breaks his finger, and Vera the Czech translator ('I suppose I'll be mentioned as the mad woman who bosses people around') is going mad and bossing people around. To an outsider, it must look like chaos: two hundred people hanging around making a lot of noise about doing not very much. But that's the nature of the beast: filming *does* require some people to hang about forever. Sikes' stunt double, for example, was picked up with the costume and make-up departments at 5.40 in the morning. It's now 2 p.m. and all he's done is rig the harness that will support him when he plunges to Bill's death. But, like nearly everyone else, he *has* to be there all day: Renny Rye may change the order of the sequences filmed and may, for instance, need his hand at 10 a.m. and the rest of his body seven hours later.

Sunlight also plays a part in dictating what will happen when. Director of photography, Walter McGill, has to be something of a magician: today's clear skies and blazing sunlight will, on screen, have to tie in with scenes supposedly shot on the same day in Oxfordshire, King's Bench Walk and Zatec. That's pretty well par for the course; what is decidedly unusual is the presence of droves of holiday-makers hauling canoes, rafts and rubber tyres out of the river and then manhandling them through the assembled crew. This phenomenon is due to the fact that the river at Chesky Krumlov curls, horseshoe-like, round the town, and that the old mill is at the end of one prong, opposite the boat-hire stand. These swimsuited people, returning their craft whence they came, are asked to remain out of sight while the cameras are rolling, but they're never out of mind. An added and unwelcome problem for 1st AD Peter Freeman, whose job during filming is to make sure everyone is where they're supposed to be, doing what they're supposed to do. And, today, that includes the visiting boat-people.

The following day is slightly easier for him. They're in the rafters of the Old Nunnery – and nobody in their right mind would want to visit. Malcolm Thornton may have been ecstatic about the dust and filth, but the rest of the crew would prefer a cleaner existence. Most of them are wearing face-masks, the temperature has soared again, it's dark and creepy and, all in all, vile. There *is* a portable air-conditioning unit, but it's like having a fan-assisted oven. It doesn't really make any difference to the roasting process.

And what happens the day after that? The temperature plummets by more than twenty degrees, it pours incessantly, and Sod's Law dictates that the crew is outside the nunnery, filming the arrival of Brownlow, Losberne and Oliver on the scene. There are also 150 extras on set (none in interloping swimsuits), two horses, a carriage and, by a stroke of luck, a stray rat. All terribly, authentically Dickensian. Add to that the haggard appearance of half of the crew, and you could be in a Cruikshank drawing.

Adding the Magic

A small point, this, but nothing written thus far has addressed how a film is really made. Alan Bleasdale's script; Keith Thompson's vision; the creative departments' look; Renny Rye's interpretation; the input of roughly another hundred people: all would count for nothing if the person in the cutting room didn't know what he or she was doing. That person is the editor, in this case David Rees. And until he gets his hands on the material that has been shot, none of it really makes sense. There is no film, no drama: just hours and hours – 49 hours in *Oliver Twist* – of single shots. It's David's job to cut them and put them together.

That is a necessarily simplistic explanation – the director has an enormous input; so does the producer; the director of photography is crucial when it comes to post-production; and all sorts of people are involved in dubbing and adding music and effects. But it is David Rees, back in the barracks at Barrandov, who cuts the film.

David always lags 24 hours behind everyone else; a reflection not on his mental acuity but on the fact that he has to wait for the previous day's 'rushes'. Rushes are like new-born babies; people invariably refer to them in reverential tones and refuse to believe they've got the celluloid equivalent of two arms and two legs until they've seen them. Which is tough for most people, because they're only seen by a few. Like new-borns, they're delivered as quickly and painlessly as is feasible. As David explains, 'they're with the editor as soon as humanely possible after the shoot because everyone [read the producer and director] is extremely keyed-up to know that the previous day went well. There are all sorts of things that can go wrong: fogging, focusing, camera tracking to name but a few...'

Happily, all sorts of things rarely go wrong, and those that do can usually be remedied during editing or in post-production, and the rushes (so called because they're 'rushed' off the negative and are not properly graded – in the US they're called 'dailies') can be edited. Equally important, any actors waiting for 'rushes clearance' can be released if they were due to fly home that day. The word 'released' is chosen advisedly: in many ways actors are pampered – but they're also prisoners.

David sets to work on those rushes. The technicalities are beyond the scope of this book (and its writer), but it is the creative process that fascinates most. The rushes show exactly what was filmed the day before. Watching it happening was like watching paint dry, but when you're looking at the rushes, you're one stage further on. A crude analogy would be that the paint has dried, the pictures are stacked against the wall, and you're wondering how to hang them. The potential is there for a startling visual feast: you just have to know how to realise that potential. It probably helps if, like David, you've edited more than seventy films.

Take the rushes of Mr Bumble making a pass at Mrs Mann in the Workhouse. The latter is holding the infant Oliver and looking at the pictures of her late husband on the wall. There are close-ups of Julie Walters half-profile to the camera; of her facing the camera; there are wide shots of the room showing all its occupants; there is David Ross from one angle, then from another; there are shots of David as Julie is speaking, and vice versa. There are, in short, a plethora of shots from which to craft a scene that will enthral, entertain, inform the viewer of what is happening – and be visually stunning. But how to choose which shot to use, which to lose, and which to place in an order that will fulfil the above criteria? David already has a great deal of written information from Renny Rye and Sam Donovan, telling him which take was NG (no good) and why; which take was partially good, which scene was 'picked-up' from the point at which it went wrong (something that rarely happens with Renny Rye; he prefers to reshoot a scene from the beginning if it goes wrong – it means the actors go back to the original positions they rehearsed). That information is invaluable to David – so is his one golden rule: 'I probably break it most of the time, but I think that for every edit to work there has to be a *purpose* to it.'

As in?

'Well, I wanted to start this scene with the close-up of Mrs Mann. We're coming in from a wide shot and a close-up seems sensible. But then you have to think of the viewers: they don't know where Mrs Mann *is*. So it's now important to tell them that she's in her sitting-room, looking at the portraits of her late husband; holding baby Oliver – and that Mr Bumble is with her. So it makes much more sense to start with the wide shot.'

That, in turn, should make sense to the reader. If it doesn't, hark back to the number of times you've said 'How did he get there?', 'That doesn't follow' or, simply, 'I don't understand...' Writers like to think they've made everything clear and that the fault lies with the director or editor. There are, of course, the (very) few occasions when the writer simply fails to explain what's going on.

Editing, particularly during post-production, becomes more complex – and often bizarre. Assistant editor Tom Kinnersley explains that 'when it comes to adding the music and effects track, the editors have all sorts of ruses. They have what's called a "sandpit" divided into sections full of all sorts of unbelievably peculiar objects; pebbles for horses' hooves; coconuts for door knocks; silk to rub near the microphone for the rustle of clothes and, for footsteps in the snow, they embed a microphone in cotton wool and then walk on it...' The people who add these effects are, appropriately, called footsteps editors, and they recreate every single sound all over again. 'The argument,' says David Rees, 'is that you don't need to re-do everything for the English dub because some of the sounds are already on the dialogue track. But you've got all that recreation on tap should you need it: the sounds that are on the dialogue track are sometimes not very distinct.' And some of them are distinctly strange. When, for example, Oliver is shot during the burglary of the Chertsey house, the gun-fire on the dialogue track is a pathetic pop – it's distorted by the film speed and has to be re-dubbed.

Sometimes the most authentic sounds are lost when a film is being dubbed into a foreign language. The sound of someone inhaling a cigarette, for example, is perfect on the dialogue track. But that track has to be lost, and with it the original sound of the inhalation. But then smoking is bad for you anyway.

After David Rees has cut the rushes, Renny Rye rushes to see them (usually in his lunch hour). He's perfectly entitled to rip them to pieces, but the chances are he won't. 'If any editor is worth his salt,' says David, '70 or 80 per cent of his cut will remain at the end of the day. And, understandably, a director won't work with an editor he's never used before.'

David Rees in the cutting-room. He, the editor, is the man who transforms multiple takes of people doing not very much rather slowly into that pacy, coherent and fluid thing called drama.

One of the loveliest shots of Oliver – and one of the best examples of the use of special effects. Viewers see this shot on screen – and then the camera pans to reveal a panorama of London behind the log. In reality, there are only a few rather peeved-looking cows. Illusion, in the shape of a photographic still lifted from an old children's encyclopaedia and inserted into the frame, creates the London of Dickens' day.

It's just as well that Renny and David have worked together before because, according to Renny, 'I know exactly how I would edit what we've shot – but I won't tell the editor. If you've got a good editor they'll find a way to cut and I love to see the way they've done it: 60 or 70 per cent of the time a brilliant editor will come up with the same – or better – instinctively. I always want to see what their instinct says. If you're in tune with the editor, and if they're good, they'll find things you haven't thought of. The whole point of running a team,' he finishes, 'is that you must use their talents properly. I don't believe in telling other people how to do their jobs. You don't hire people – you work with them.'

Renny's own job, like David's, is a mixture of the technical and the creative. As regards the latter, 'you're looking for that magic moment in every single shot – and sometimes you get them on take one. That's always a huge pleasure for a director.' Renny goes on to discuss a scene which, as usual, he's planned in his head and which, on the day, nearly gave him cold feet. 'Timing-wise it was a really tricky thing to attempt. I was thinking I should have found another way of doing it. I was setting myself up for trouble.'

It's the scene of Monks falling out of a tree during an argument with Fagin – and it worked like a dream on the first take. It looks simple, but it's hugely complicated and could have presented a nightmare for continuity. Think close-ups, wide shots, cutting to Fagin then to Monks, stunt doubles, the tree branch rigged on a pivoting axis, and the probability of having to shoot the scene fifteen times. After the close-up of Marc Warren (Monks) in the tree, Marc climbed down and then lay in the ditch below as the stunt double took his place. The subsequent wide shot is of the double, and the last 'I'm not coming down' before he falls is actually the double's voice. Bearing in mind they're only using one camera, it's essential for the tree branch to break and the double to fall at exactly the moment they cut to a close-up of Fagin walking past. The purpose of this shot is not to show Fagin, it's to block the sight of Marc Warren in the ditch. 'And the stuntman,' adds Renny, 'has to roll far enough and fast enough so that he's out of the frame by the time we pan round to Marc getting to his feet.'

Could have been nasty. Worked like a dream.

Monks was doubled again when he fell off his horse as he and Mrs Leeford were casing the Fleming joint. It's a funny scene – he's bending down to try to establish the sex of his mount – but it could have been fraught. And, in the end, it did require several takes. Part of the problem is that the horse wrangler had to remain with the animal until seconds before the camera starts to roll (Marc Warren would be the first to admit to his unfamiliarity with horses), and also that the substitution of the double and the subsequent fall has to be a fluid action. One of the takes – rejected by Renny – was spectacular, but rather more James Bond than *Oliver Twist*. The stuntman hurled himself at Lindsay Duncan's horse, bounced back off it against his own horse and then crashed to the ground. Lindsay Duncan handled the situation with great aplomb, but the take was far too violent to use.

Stuntmen apart, there are other, less obvious forms of visual trickery involved in making *Oliver Twist*. The scene of Oliver sleeping under a fallen tree as he makes his way to London for example, is a classic. The camera retreats from the sleeping Oliver to take a wide shot, revealing a panoramic scene of London above the tree. Given that the scene was filmed in Oxfordshire (and that panoramic views of London invariably involve neon lights and tower blocks), the backdrop is fake. It's a still from an ancient children's encyclopaedia and is inserted into the shot by visual effects supervisor Dennis Lowe. Ditto the seaside town towards which Agnes stumbles at the beginning of Episode One. And likewise with the ships' masts in the background when we first meet Fagin in that same episode. The scene was filmed in the Czech town of Kolin which, like the rest of the Czech Republic, is nowhere near the sea.

Dennis Lowe also applied his magic touch to Agnes after she'd given birth to Oliver and died. A little tell-tale pulse in her neck betrayed the fact that she was only playing dead, so Dennis erased the pulse in post-production. You can subject actors to all manner of indignities under the auspices of art, but decorum dictates that you shouldn't really kill them.

1 | **Jug-Loops:** Small curly hairpieces worn by women.
Mittings: Shirts.
Newgate Knockers: Not what you're thinking.
They're the robust facial sideboards of Victoriana.

Costume and Make-up

Jug-Loops, Mittings and Newgate Knockers [1]

Oliver's mother Agnes (Sophia Myles), unwittingly advertising IKEA. The creative departments envisaged her as a fresh country girl (which is just as well considering she has half of the countryside splattered all over her). 'I hope,' said Sophia, 'it looks as good – or rather as bad – as it felt. Gruesome scene after gruesome scene...'

Continuity is the key to many productions, and this dress was no exception. Here, Agnes is stumbling towards the seaside town where she dies in childbirth. The dying, however, was filmed six weeks after the stumbling, but both Agnes and her dress had to look as if hours, not weeks, had passed. Happily, Sophia came back to life again. The dress didn't.

There are many words that spring to mind when one thinks of costumes for a period drama. Empire gowns, perhaps. Or tunics. Tail-coats. The odd bonnet. But the last word anyone would ever associate with a Dickens' production is IKEA, the modern Swedish superstore best known for sofas. Yet that is precisely the word uttered by Ros Ebbutt, costume designer on *Oliver Twist*.

'Oh yes,' she repeats. 'The fabric for that dress of Agnes came from IKEA. £1 per metre.' Surely Ros was there shopping for a sofa and just happened upon that fabric by chance? 'Oh no. I went on a specific shopping trip for *Oliver Twist*. I was looking for stuff which had exactly the sort of fine weave that's typically early nineteenth century. It was white when I bought it. I knew it would dye well and I created the pattern by using those little blocks that I bought in India. To buy enough ready-patterned muslin of the right kind from a specialist place would cost a fortune.'

It's that level of knowledge, that sort of confidence, combined with over two decades of experience, that has earned Ros her reputation – and her BAFTA awards and nominations for *Tom Jones*, *The Tenant of Wildfell Hall* and *Vanity Fair*. This lady knows whereof she speaks.

Then she's off again, combing through the 25 racks of clothes that constitute the *Oliver Twist* wardrobe. Phrases like 'I bought this in Shepherd's Bush', 'I found this in India', 'This was inspired by an Ingres portrait' and 'I was thinking of neoclassical paintings by Alma-Tadema and Leighton' trip off her tongue, as she talks through the genesis of her costumes.

The layman (well, this man) may wonder what all the fuss is about. There have been umpteen productions set in the 1820s and '30s; so many paintings, films and references – and enough adaptations of *Oliver Twist* – to help with the costuming process. Surely all one has to do is make Fagin look shifty, plonk the girls in pink meringues and shove a bonnet on Mrs Bedwin and no-one would bat an eyelid. Which, of course, is absolutely true. No-one would look twice.

'It's not that I want people to go, "Oh gosh, what fantastic costumes" – anything but,' explains Ros. 'I want people to believe that the characters they're watching are real people. That's what I'm paid to do.'

Then, rather spookily – and seemingly unaware of the fact – Ros begins to talk about them as if they are real. Rifling through the racks of clothes for Fagin's den, she pounces on an old coat. 'This is one of the things Fagin found. He had these garments he made up himself and amongst them is a battered old eighteenth-century man's dressing gown. He's converted it into his magic coat by putting a bit of a cloak in the back.' Having – appropriately – conjured Fagin into life, Ros moves on to his headgear. 'I was looking and looking and looking for a hat and then I thought, well, Fagin found an old tricorn that had collapsed. I think it's an old cardinal's hat. If it has collapsed a bit then you can get a really interesting shape, you can push one side up or down and you get a hat that isn't any shape we know. Fagin, if you remember, came from Czechoslovakia, so it's entirely appropriate that he's got all these things that we don't necessarily identify with. He's got quite a cosmopolitan look.'

Fagin (Robert Lindsay). 'We're looking at several different worlds,' says Costume Designer Ros Ebbutt. 'And what I've done with Fagin and his world is to give him racks and rails of stuff that's been stolen – because that's one of the things they do. They couldn't sell the more gaudy stuff, so they used it for themsleves. It means one's got the opportunity to do all these combinations.'

Long before Ros came on the scene, Alan Bleasdale had determined that Fagin should be identified by his foreign-ness – not by his being a Jew. By sheer coincidence, he decided that Fagin originally came from Prague – at least six months before the decision was made to film in Prague.

The discussion about Fagin continues, and one almost expects him to creep out from behind one of the racks or, more likely, to be plotting to steal Mrs Leeford's expensive wardrobe. 'She's the only one with any real pretensions to fashion,' says Ros. 'When we first meet her she's living in Paris, well beyond her means, probably on credit, buying her expensive clothes and trying to maintain her household. Paris fashions were ahead of English ones so she's got these lower waistlines, relatively large sleeves and big hats, whereas the English women would be less exaggerated.' Ros pauses for breath (this doesn't happen a lot). 'Well, Mrs Leeford is particularly exaggerated.' (Alan Bleasdale's stage directions describe her clothes as 'the 1820s version of power-dressing'.) As if to prove the point, Ros pulls a hugely dramatic, Cruella de Ville red-and-black number from the rail. 'This,' she says with a flourish, 'is the murdering dress.' High-necked, wide-shouldered and beautifully embroidered, it has a matching feathered hat that could commit a few little crimes on its own. (Director Renny Rye later explains that hats are a godsend for him – they frame the face and add another dimension to close-ups.) This outfit is, of course, the one Mrs Leeford wears for her special day – the murder of her husband.

Like all the outfits in this series, it wasn't just conjured out of thin air, and has a suitably exotic background. 'There's an Ingres portrait of a woman in black,' explains Ros, 'with an incredibly high neck and a big hat. That was part of the inspiration. I also looked at a Bronzino portrait of a woman poisoner – wrong period but I wanted an element of the Borgias in Mrs Leeford. Another Ingres also gave me a clue for the dress she wears when she wallops Brownlow with her stick. The one with the enormous scalloped neck. It's really quite extreme. I found some old Italian millinery velvet in Brick Lane and piped the collar with magenta silk, which I just happened to have.'

Ros is endlessly fascinating about her sources of both inspiration and material. But what also emerges from her conversation is that absolute necessity for her to believe in the reality of the characters. Talking of Fagin as if he really exists may, to an outsider, sound contrived and even a little arch, the bottom line is that he does exist – and Ros is one of the people who created him.

Mrs Leeford (Lindsay Duncan) in her murderous prime and, right, in her final decline. Lindsay Duncan jokes of the latter that 'there will come a day when they won't be able to plaster over the cracks and I'll look like that anyway…' That's highly unlikely: apart from the fact that Lindsay Duncan isn't a raddled arthritic alcoholic, she doesn't have the services of Make-up Designer Lesley Lamont-Fisher constantly at hand to age her ten years; to transform her from Mrs Leeford's stern beauty into a haggard hell-hag.

'Their history is vital to us,' she says. 'We have conversations about their backgrounds – and it's got nothing to do with the viewers. It helps us if we can create an amalgam that actually looks like society and not cartoons or fashion shoots. They should look like people who are bringing their baggage – of any type – with them. And we must make the actors feel completely that they are these people. They must feel at ease with what they're wearing.'

The input from the actors themselves is also vital. 'Artists, quite rightly, don't like having things imposed on them. You should discuss it with them first and not just say, "Right, that's you." Anyway,' she adds with a laugh, 'I've given up doing too much preparation for characters before you know who's going to be cast. You can have an idea in your head for someone who's tall and blonde and, of course, they end up casting someone who's short and dark. And there are colours which look wonderful on some people and simply don't suit others. I once designed wonderful golden dresses for an actress and she looked ghastly, I mean ghastly, in gold. Shooting was already underway but I had to say we've got to rethink this completely. We did – and I thought that's the last time I'm ever going to get into that situation.' (This is about the fourth time Ros has used the word 'completely'. It's an interesting insight into her own character. No half-measures here.)

'The thing about all the characters,' she continues, 'is that they're on a journey: they're coming from somewhere and they're going somewhere.' And she means figuratively as well as literally. Mrs Leeford is making a journey through a life that contained so much hope and ends in such bitter disappointment. 'She's always stylish,' explains Ros, 'but when she goes into confrontations she's always dressed up to the nines. Even when she ages she's still making the very best of herself, so I've followed the fashions. It's all rather exaggerated and, for example, the dress that she wears in her final confrontation with Brownlow is slightly unsuitable for an ageing woman with arthritis.

the murder dress

top, a Parish Beadle of the day and, **bottom,** Mr Bumble (David Ross) as a Beadle incarnate. The uniform is almost identical. So is the pomposity (of Mr Bumble, that is).

Leeford, of course, makes an actual journey. He goes to Rome, so his clothes become looser and lighter. I'm glad we filmed that in Marienbad and not in England, because in England you're always trying to hide the umbrellas keeping the rain off the parasols.

'I actually had to look into what men wore in spas in those days. I found some photos from the 1860s – not the right period as the camera hadn't been invented in the 20s – with men lounging about wearing these deeply unattractive, dreadful-looking drawstring baggy knickers, and I thought "Oh God I can't put Mr Leeford into these terrible things." So, for decency's sake, I had these flesh-coloured lycra underpants made and we've evolved a little, sort of wrap-over loincloth, which looks quite nice. We also had some toga-like cloak things which they can wrap around them. I was thinking of these Victorian neoclassical paintings of people draping themselves in pools. Rather romantic.'

Later Ros digs out the paintings she's talking about. They're actually rather pornographic: men and women lolling about with very little on, looking meaningfully at snakes and bits of fruit.

Even the characters in *Oliver Twist* who appear to be static are making journeys. Mrs Mann is ever hopeful that Mr Slout will die and she will rise to run the Workhouse on her own. 'She hasn't got much money until Sea Captain Mann dies,' says Ros. 'Then she's able to buy herself slightly glitzy dresses – including the dress she wears when she marries Mr Bumble.' The material for her wedding dress, it transpires, was found in Brick Lane: '£1.50 a metre – a bit of a bargain. It's lightweight French voile and the print is so like the prints of the time.' Mrs Mann herself was partly inspired by a 'wonderful engraving of a fierce-looking Workhouse matron. For Mr Bumble there's a Cruikshank drawing and another rather nice painting by Sir David Wilkie. There was a standard beadle's uniform so there isn't much leeway.' (There is, actually, if you're Ros. From her own personal store of materials she added an early nineteenth-century fabric that she's used to give Bumble a rather flashy and individual handkerchief, which blends in perfectly with the uniform – and Bumble's vanity.)

Costume Designer Ros Ebbutt throttling Julie Walters.

They're in the mobile wardrobe, containing only the costumes needed for that day. And today is an easy day (perhaps that's why Ros is giggling). On one memorable day she and her assistants had to dress people from different decades in Paris, Rome and London at six in the morning in a tent in the middle of a thunderstorm. 'It was hideous,' says Ros, unconsciously tightening her grip on the blameless Julie. 'Absolutely hideous.'

However, Mrs Mann and Mr Bumble's days of snappy dressing are numbered. They end up as Workhouse inmates, wearing the Workhouse uniform. These uniforms were described as 'singularly ugly and disfiguring'. For obvious reasons, Ros hasn't made her Workhouse uniforms disfiguring, but she has ensured that everything in the post-1834 Workhouse is in 'shades of grey'.

Funnily enough, her wardrobe store could probably double as a Workhouse. Deep in the bowels of one of the monolithic buildings that constitute Barrandov Studios in Prague, it's in startling contrast to the bright, boiling summer's day outside where, during a break in filming, some of the actors are taking time out. Annette Crosbie, after spending all morning pouring tea in Brownlow's drawing room, is now drinking tea from a plastic cup and eating a Czech doughnut in the shade. Michael Kitchen, in the full glare of the sun, is complaining about being too hot in his frock-coat. 'Last time you were too cold,' says a merrily dismissive Ros. He wasn't the only one.'Last time' was five weeks previously in England, when it was freezing. Now it's nearly 100 degrees. Michael Kitchen shrugs off his heavy frock-coat and sits down. 'Stripping your clothes off is an incredibly modern phenomenon,' muses Ros. 'People then would have thought it an extraordinary thing to do, to actually choose to go and broil yourself in the sun.' Michael Kitchen points out – with some justification – that he's in the middle of Central Europe where summer is infinitely hotter that it ever was in Dickensian London. 'Well,' says Ros, 'they still wouldn't have taken their clothes off.'

The conversation becomes an exchange of good-humoured banter – but it does reveal another piece of interesting information. 'No-one would ever have dreamed of wearing expensive fabrics next to their skin,' explains Ros. 'All their undergarments would have been linen and then cotton, when it came in later in the century. Men had a sort of knee-length garment, which turns into the shirt we have today. Our lot (on *Oliver Twist*) would probably have had some sort of drawstring garment as well. Or the shirts could wrap under the crotch so that it was all very comfy.' It actually sounds hideously uncomfortable, but this doesn't seem quite the moment to ask Michael Kitchen if he's into method acting in the nether region department.

Then, as always happens on sets, someone comes running up to an actor, in this case Annette Crosbie, telling her she's needed on set. They're running late so they're going to kill two birds with one stone. Annette is needed for the last take of this scene and for the next scene. Both are shot in Brownlow's drawing room – ten years apart. In the first she's pouring tea (again) in the 1820s, and we only see her hands and midriff. To save time between takes, the make-up department is going to change Annette's wig now, ready for the 1830s shot where we see her entire body. Just a small example of everything not being as it seems on screen.

If there's one department that knows all about everything not being as it seems, it's the make-up crew. They are responsible for turning the glowingly healthy Sam Smith into the pallid Oliver, for applying 'Death' make-up to the tanned Czech children who become workhouse inmates, for transforming the luminous Lindsay Duncan into the compellingly malignant Mrs Leeford, for disguising Robert Lindsay under Fagin and, perhaps most extreme of all, for turning Marc Warren into the character of Monks.

Top left: The 'Death' range of make-up is constantly used on Oliver. The talented yet disembodied hand of Lesley Lamont-Fisher applies the grim reaper to the naturally rosebud lips of Oliver (Sam Smith). She's already greased-down his springy blond hair and done away with the healthy glow that normally accompanies Sam Smith.

Bottom left: The Czech extras who play Oliver's fellow Workhouse inmates have been dealt with in a similar fashion. Most of them were incredibly tanned – until Lesley and her assistant Chris Redman got their hands on them. They didn't object to that – but several of them objected to the gruel in their bowls and imported their own sandwiches. This was not a wise idea.

Above: Chris Redman and Monks (Marc Warren) staring into each other's eyes. Mark's left eye is, in fact, being given a David Bowie type makeover: Monks has one blue and one brown eye whereas Marc's are both blue.

Below: Lesley applies fake scars to Monks' knuckles.

Brick Lane. 'So,' continues Ros, 'he's a bit like the romantic bogeyman. Also, because he's lived abroad a lot and has a bit of money, it's pretty fashionable stuff, if slightly decadent. He'd be the equivalent of a romantic French drug-taking poet if he didn't have all that awful baggage.'

Initial thoughts about Marc Warren being exactly like the character he plays are dispelled when, during another break in filming, he emerges into the sunshine with Sam Smith and proceeds to show him a few card tricks. Then they go off to play with Sam's Frisbee – a game that nearly ends in disaster when Sam almost decapitates Sophia Myles. Sophia isn't due to die until the following day, so it would be a little inconvenient if she perished now. Especially as she's supposed to die whilst giving birth to Sam.

Lesley looks over to Marc and says, 'He's actually blond, you know. We had to dye his hair because short wigs can look a bit dodgy and we decided that the younger Monks would look a bit rattish. When he's older he wears a wig; the longer, more romantic look which poets would have worn. Marc's got a very good bone structure so the longer hair really suits him. Also, he's played a policeman before [in The Vice] and we wanted to get totally away from that.' One could safely say that they've succeeded.

The transformation is complete. 'It's the only job I've done where you go into make-up for ages and end up looking worse than before. But after doing something like this, you know you'll never get it again...'

Actor Andy Serkis was transformed into the gin-sodden Bill Sikes by make-up designer Lesley Lamont-Fisher. Lesley's biggest consideration was, in fact, the alcohol problem of the day and its effect on the physiognomies of the characters in *Oliver Twist*. London was awash with gin. Kate Norbury, Alan Bleasedale's researcher, found statistics for the total attendance in London's fourteen leading gin shops in 1833. They read, frighteningly, as follows: Men, 142,453; Women, 108,593; Children, 11,494.

Much later – and, appropriately, over drinks in a Prague bar – Lesley is recalling one of the major aspects of the *Oliver Twist* look. 'One of the things I had to consider on this is the gin problem of the period. Gin was extremely cheap and they swigged it a lot.' She's not exaggerating. In 1834, a Select Committee on Drunkenness reported that 'these are the marks by which to know the regular gin-drinker: livid cheeks, deep wrinkles, bloodshot eyes, brown teeth or white gums without teeth, skin and bone, shaking hands, sore legs, creeping palsy, a hacking cough, rags, filth and stench.' And no messing about with ice and slice: they drank it neat or with a little hot water.

Lesley really went to town to create the Sikes look. She's given him heavy dark sideboards, hacked at his hair so that it's all askew, given him a scar that looks as if it's from a broken bottle, added broken veins and dirtied him down. 'I've done a lot of work with alcoholics and street people in the past,' says Lesley,'and it's funny because after I've made up Andy I can actually smell him; I imagine that appalling odour is there even when it's not. A lot of other people have said that to me as well. There's that look, that really unpleasant look. He just doesn't wash. It was a very smelly period anyway. We forget that with all our deodorants.'

On the opposite end of the spectrum from Sikes is Mrs Leeford. If she smelled at all it would be of some wicked scent (Joan Collins would be promoting it nowadays). Although she has a drink problem of her own, one can't imagine her reeking of the stuff. And, when we first meet her, she's all Parisian chic. There is, funnily enough, an eighteenth-century reference to Parisian hygiene, in which one R. Phene Spiers declares that 'The French use very little water, and believing they can wash themselves with the corner of a towel, they do not see the necessity for a bath.' Oh well...Mrs Leeford isn't actually French.

Mrs Leeford in the 1820s (inset) and, main picture, ten years on. 'Of all the character who have grown ten years older,' writes Alan Bleasdale in his stage directions, 'she is the one who has suffered the most, and at twice the pace. Wheezing, arthritic, on a walking stick, and heavily made-up in a travesty for her former self. But if the body is gone, the spirit remains. The spirit being, inevitably, gin.'

But she is – in the shape of Lindsay Duncan. The very blonde Lindsay has undergone a huge transformation in Lesley's hands. 'I don't like blonde hair very much in period productions: partly because you see very few paintings of blondes and partly because they couldn't really bleach their hair with any degree of success. You could get a good henna colour and a good black, but it wasn't really until the 1960s that the bleaching process became more sophisticated.

'We've taken Lindsay into a soft red for the first part to make her look as attractive as possible – then she really goes to seed in the second half. She's hennaed her hair – this lovely red colour which makes her more fiery, but of course the roots are showing, she puts on too much make-up, pencils her eyebrows and darkens her lips, so the whole thing is over the top. She's fighting to keep her looks and to disguise her blotchy, alcoholic face but it's just not working. It's fun to do because Lindsay's a really attractive actress – and a really good one. Like a lot of really good artists she has the courage to push a performance and a character; to go beyond a cliché and aim for the truth. And it's hard for some artists because I don't like eye make-up on a period piece. It's difficult for some actresses to have that nude look, but it's correct for this. You can actually date some films by the make-up the actors are wearing, which is outrageous. If you look at the paintings they're not wearing any mascara or eyeliner.' So, the later Mrs Leeford apart (she's a law unto herself), no-one is wearing eye make-up. Instead, they have their eyelashes dyed to provide definition for the camera.

The beauty of the make-up department is that its effects are more than skin-deep. Again and again one hears actors, particularly those with quite extreme make-up, say that their make-up puts them straight into character. Marc Warren says that as soon Lesley puts the brown contact lens with the dilated pupil into his eye, he becomes Monks. Sophia Myles ('every time there's a rain machine, mud or misery I know it's for me') says that looking appalling all the time helps her identify with the wretched, hapless Agnes. 'The greatest compliment to me and to costume,' says Lesley, 'is when an actor says the look of the character frees them up for the emotion of the character. Take Sophia, for instance. She said it helped her that she looked as if she'd been crying for hours. That was quite fun to do.' Sounding for a moment like Mrs Leeford, she launches into a robust explanation of how to make Sophia look suicidal. 'You just sit her down, break her face down and blow menthol vapour into her eyes to make her look as if she's been crying for hours. Then she looks at herself and she looks pathetic, sad and miserable, and as if she's been out in the elements for hours – and she hasn't even opened her mouth.'

Acting's all glamour, then.

The costume and make-up departments don't only work with each other. At the initial stages of planning, they work in tandem with Malcolm Thornton, the Production Designer. As Lesley points out, 'There's no use me making Monks a certain way and then, when you see his house, having the viewer think there's no way that character would live there.' Meticulous planning goes into matching the character to the environment: Mrs Leeford is supremely chic in her elegant Paris apartment, but fading fast in her shabbier London abode. The Workhouse 'shades of grey' described by Ros extend to the interior and exterior of the building – to the 'Death' make-up of the inmates, and to the Baby Farm. As Malcolm Thornton puts it, 'we wanted to give the impression that the only colour Oliver saw in the first ten years of Oliver's life was in Mr Bumble's uniform.' Then there's the gaudy, grimy world of Fagin. The den is just identifiable as a Georgian interior, and some of the clothes date back to that time as well. Ros has based her ideas on the fact that most of the clothing is 'fifth-, sixth- or even seventh-hand', so could span several generations. And Lesley and Malcolm, because they 'lived like rats' (Fagin's lot, that is), added several generations of filth to faces and building alike. Ros points out that the first time we catch a glimpse of Fagin is actually in the year of Oliver's birth, and 'I was able to go even further back with the costumes for that'. It's a market scene in Episode One, full of strolling players, puppeteers and magicians – described in Alan Bleasdale's stage directions as 'Breughel comes to life'. So the look here is deliberately highly cosmopolitan, with some costumes dating back to the time of the French Revolution. 'After all,' says Ros, '1789 was only thirty years previously; a lot of the players have come from abroad, so there would have been a huge range of styles.'

Leeford

Mrs Leeford

Nancy

Fagin
as
Levinski

Costume Designer Ros Ebbutt's fabulous collages that show the evolution of some of the principal characters. Colours and fabrics as well as designs are vital to the genesis of every single character.

'Mrs Leeford,' says Ros, 'is really the only one who has any pretentions to fashion.' And here **(top right)** she's sketched at the height of Parisian chic – big sleeves, a high neck and an A-line dress.

Nancy **(bottom left)**, whose clothes are something of a hotch-potch, obviously can't match her for modernity. Her dress has a higher waist, an indication that it's probably second-hand – harking-back to the Empire line so familiar from Jane Austen's heroines.

Leeford **(top left)** is in a frock-coat appropriate to the fashion of the day whilst what we see of Fagin's waistcoat matches that of a tail-coat – much more old-fashioned. So, of course, are his knee-breeches.

'The history of the characters,' says Ros, 'is vital to us. We've got to make these people look like real people, bringing their baggage – of whatever type – with them.'

The same amount of planning has gone into the seemingly staid world of Brownlow. Dickens is closely identified with the high Victorian era, but *Oliver Twist* was set in the reign of William IV. The furniture in Brownlow's town house is contemporary rather than antique, and the clothes reflect the characters' ages. Like Fagin, Brownlow and Mrs Bedwin would have been born in the eighteenth century, so they've brought some of that era with them. 'Brownlow,' illustrates Ros, 'starts with a tail-coat and then, when we move on ten years, we put him into a frock-coat. The changing shape of the waistcoats is also a handy frame of reference to the passing of time.' By this time wigs had gone out of fashion (partly because of the French Revolution and partly because of a powder tax), but people – especially men – wore their hair short. 'Underneath their wigs,' explains Lesley, 'people were bald or had very short hair, so the classical look came in for men. They started to brush it forward [think Nero] and that gradually evolved into the sideboards.' From then on, facial hair flourished, producing the mutton-chops, the moustache and then the flowing beard. 'The women would have had their own hair as well,' says Lesley, 'although they would have little hairpieces with curls. It was particularly difficult to keep curls, so they'd just pop a little curly piece on the front.'

At that point, Sophia Myles approaches. No cute curly pieces for her: she's in windswept, weatherbeaten mode – and is on her way to give birth to Oliver. She shot the run-up to the birth six weeks previously (redefining the concept of a long labour), and is back in the dress that survived her flailing on the edge of a cliff and falling in mud. She's asked if she's aware of the provenance of that dress. She isn't – and seems genuinely aghast when told it comes from the place that sells sofas. Then she giggles. 'Right: we'll have to re-shoot. I am not standing on a cliff in an IKEA sofa cover!'

chapter 5

Cast and Characters

Fagin ·•· Robert Lindsay

Robert Lindsay is standing in the middle of Fagin's den – otherwise known as the dismal attic of the Old Nunnery in Chesky Krumlov. The heat is stifling, 90° and rising, but he's wearing several layers of clothing, topped by Fagin's voluminous coat. There are about 30 people in front of him, hanging onto his every word and watching every move he makes. Well, you think, that's normal. That's acting.

But what an act. Robert is speaking in Czech, a language unfamiliar to him. Furthermore, he's got to remember to maintain the rhythms and inflections of Fagin's voice. Vera, the interpreter, is standing to his right, just out of shot, checking his pronunciation. So, silently, are half the film crew. He's speaking in their native language. And everyone is watching what he's doing. Yes, he's 'just acting' – being Fagin. But he's also performing a magic trick. A real one.

'I was a bit nervous yesterday,' says Robert the following day. 'It was the scene where Fagin's going a bit mad: Bill's just told him he's killed Nancy. There I was tying knots in scarves and producing watches and whatnot, speaking in Czech and trying to get the magic together in one take while the camera was closing in on me...' Then Robert grins. 'But I'm having a ball. It's the most fantastic part to play.'

Robert Lindsay is familiar with the part of Fagin, albeit from a different interpretation. He recently played the part at the London Palladium, but as the sort of singing Shylock familiar from the Lionel Bart musical. This Fagin, as everyone now knows, is different.

'Fagin will always attract controversy, however you play him. The press will probably say that Alan Bleasdale has gone all politically correct, but even Dickens panicked about the anti-Semitic aspect.' (He actually apologised and subsequently removed derogatory references to 'The Jew'.) 'And,' continues Robert, 'the Guinness thing [in the David Lean film] was appalling...shocking. I mean it was brilliantly acted, but you just couldn't do that nowadays. That aside, I don't think Alec Guinness's character would have been attractive to children.'

That is the essence of Fagin. 'He's charismatic; children are just completely overwhelmed by him. What's important about this Fagin is that he's a wandering magician, a street entertainer. He's roamed through the European capitals and ends up in London. And children are just fascinated by him. He lures them in. Then – there's a brilliant scene which is also in the book – he tells them they must know fear. He tells them that if they leave him, they'll be hung. He even shows Oliver a book on hanging. That's the first book he ever sees – with a picture of the gallows.'

Not, then, a particularly sympathetic character. 'No. He's incredibly manipulative and scheming. But there *is* an element of sympathy with all these characters, and I suppose if there's anything redeeming about Fagin it's his love for Nancy. He absolutely *adores* that girl. If he has any love at all it's for that young girl. His relationship with her is extraordinary.

We've had all sorts of conversations about the triangular relationship between Fagin, Bill and Nancy. It's a little mystical in some way. And it's those sorts of undercurrents that make *Oliver Twist* such a great, fantastic book.'

One would imagine that Robert Lindsay's familiarity with the role of Fagin would have proved an advantage as regards this production. It proved to be quite the opposite. 'Joan Washington [the renowned voice coach] said to me that I had to wipe the slate clean; get rid of whatever it was in my brain that told me I knew how to play it.' Four or five lessons with Joan helped expunge all traces of the previous Fagin and create a new one – so did the teeth. The thoroughly nasty set of dentures do more than alter Robert's appearance: they help transform his voice. 'Fagin needs a Czech accent, which involves speaking from the front of the mouth. And Renny said would I please try to get a bit of Cockney in it. Then there's a bit of Jewish – which is a rhythm thing.' It becomes apparent that one can't just 'put on a voice'. 'It's a question of balance. You have to let all these things in, work through the various elements and let them inhabit you, as well as using yourself and your own rhythms.'

The young Artful Dodger is captivated by Fagin and his magic tricks. Alan Bleasdale envisaged Fagin as coming from Prague – and by a happy coincidence they ended up filming there. 'There's a huge tradition of magic and puppetry in Bohemia,' says Robert. 'Magic and mystery seem part of the whole culture.' Another coincidence saw Robert buying a puppet for his daughter – one that looked uncannily like Fagin.

Difficult, but learning new voices is a normal part of an actor's repertoire. Learning how to do magic tricks is not. What is so intriguing about Fagin's magic is that it's real – taught to Robert by the magician Ali Bongo (not, you'll be surprised to hear, his real name). 'Ali is adorable,' grins Robert. 'He's a historical magician and also an academic. And he's worked a lot with children...I think he had the first children's magic show on television. He came to my house almost every day for two weeks. We set up props in my sitting room: costumes, doves and God knows what. We even had explosions – my dogs were going crazy...he gave me this beautiful old Russian Christmas box full of scarves and tricks and conjuring things I've been practising with. There's no artifice about the tricks,' he continues. 'We're talking Victorian tricks that are still used. There's a thing called a casserole – basically a casserole dish. One minute it's got fire in it, the next it's got balloons and scarves and then you open it again and all these doves fly out. It's the most fantastic thing. Ali can just do it...'

Do *what*, for heaven's sake? How's it all done? But Robert Lindsay isn't telling. 'You become very protective about these things. Even with me being an amateur I don't want people to know how it's done...'

Disappointing for the nosy amongst us, but an added bonus for Robert Lindsay. If he ever loses the day job – given that he's one of Britain's most sought-after actors, this is a tad unlikely – he's got another card up his sleeve.

Mr Brownlow ⚬ Michael Kitchen

'I've told you before,' says Grimwig to Brownlow, 'this is what becomes of being good. No good ever came of it.' 'I am not a good man!' is Brownlow's vehement response. Here, Michael Kitchen captures the essence of Brownlow. He looks benevolent – yet there's something about the eyes that indicate a complex and haunted soul.

It's all glitz around here. Michael Kitchen is sitting in the catering tent on the patch of grass outside Studio 4 at Barrandov. The trestle tables and benches wouldn't go amiss in a Workhouse; someone has spilled orange juice on one of them and Michael accidentally dips his sleeve into it. Or rather, Mr Brownlow's sleeve. He's being Mr Brownlow for a very long time today: it's an extended shoot, starting at 7.30 a.m. and finishing at 10.30 p.m.

Michael Kitchen grimaces and looks at the trailing (now damp) linen sleeve. 'I'm not terribly keen on costume drama as a rule.' One of Britain's best-known TV actors, he's normally to be found in the twentieth century in, for example, the acclaimed *Reckless*. 'So many people have had a go at the classics and it's easy to fall over on them.' Then he grins. 'But this one's different. You couldn't pass up on this. The script was a revelation – a joy. I think Alan's done the book a great favour, because it suffered under the regime of *Oliver!* [the musical] – it just disappeared under the weight of it. I hope,' he adds, 'that Brownlow turns out to be as interesting as he is in this script, because it's certainly there on the page. It's just this endless quest to fulfil it.'

A quest hampered, it transpires, by a wig. 'I'm not normally at the head of the queue when the wigs are handed out,' he says with another grin. 'I'm not very comfortable in them. I mean this one *looks* great – I'd just rather it wasn't on my head.' Then he laughs. 'Well, it just comes with the territory, doesn't it?'

The territory, at the moment, is Brownlow's drawing room. It seems that a disproportionate amount of time is being spent in that room. 'I know: same place, every day. I've been in the drawing room for two weeks now.' Another grin. 'Wretched man should get out more.' But, of course, one of the reasons why he doesn't get out much is that all the interior scenes of Brownlow's London house have to be shot *en bloc* – and that means the scenes in the 1820s *and* the 1830s. Depending on the schedule, they might be doing one decade in the morning and the other in the afternoon. Furthermore, Michael Kitchen doesn't just spend a lot of time in the drawing room – he started on the second day of the shoot in March and will finish in August, on the last day. Brownlow is an enormous part – and is a fairly complex character.

In both Dickens and previous adaptations he's something of a benevolent old fuddy-duddy, but here there's a definite conflict in him. The aura of 'goodness' that surrounds him, and that others perceive in him is tempered or even belied by the fact that he is tortured by previous wrongs – by forcing Leeford into a dreadful marriage for one.

But Michael Kitchen is coy about revealing too much of what he thinks of Brownlow, or about how he's playing the character. 'I don't like mouthing off about it,' he says with an apologetic smile. 'I think the more you talk about it, the less gets across.' Fair enough: one could hardly complain about saving that mesmerising, mellifluous voice for playing Brownlow, rather than talking about him.

Mrs Mann ·•· Julie Walters

Spare a thought for one of Britain's most famous actresses: she's been flying in and out of Prague like a yo-yo; being Mrs Mann one day, a Russian Princess the next – and Julie Walters in the bits squeezed in between. 'Yes – God help me. I'm doing two films at once. The other one's an American film based on a Turgenev and a Chekhov story rolled into one. It could have been a lot more awkward, actually, because in terms of period there's only about twenty years' difference.' Julie looks at herself in the mirror (nothing do with vanity – she's in make-up) and pats her wig. 'The Russian Princess is mad – mad exploding hair as well. It says in the novel "her head was uncovered" and I was shocked at that...she's meant to be a princess, so not *quite* the same as Mrs Mann – but even Mrs Mann wouldn't go about with her head uncovered.' Then Julie looks down her nose. 'Mind you, she's not a *real* aristocrat. She married into it – and everyone thinks she's rather vulgar.' A rare pause for breath, and then a wicked grin. 'The part stretched me.'

This is classic Julie Walters; rattling along at high speed, throwing out cracking good stories, laughing at herself, putting on 'voices' and making faces. It's a truly wonderful performance. It's also a classic 'avoidance' technique: give a journalist good copy and they're less likely to try to dig for dirt. One isn't sure if Julie Walters is actually doing this deliberately, but as one highly-regarded journalist said: 'Who cares? All most of us want is a good story – and Julie Walters *is good*.'

Julie is a stalwart of the Alan Bleasdale 'team'. She doesn't just act in his dramas – he writes parts specifically with her in mind. As he does with, amongst others, Lindsay Duncan, Robert Lindsay and David Ross. As if on cue, David Ross walks into the room. He and Julie have acted together on numerous occasions and, according to David, 'I've had my eye on you for ages. Now I've finally got you and we both end up in the Workhouse.'

'Yes but that's your fault – dragging Mrs Mann down over that bloody locket business.'

'They're both as bad as each other.'

opposite: Mrs Mann in her prime and, **above**, as a destitute workhouse inmate of ten years later. 'Dickens was so passionate,' says Alan Bleasdale. 'He wrote these wonderfully comic scenes with Mrs Mann and Mr Bumble, but he also had a fierce desire to try to change society. And one of the ways he tried was to show there are always consequences to your actions.' And the consequences for Mrs Mann are, quite rightly, dire. The weather had it in for her as well: the snow in the above photograph wasn't scripted. It's real – a rare occasion of the elements enhancing the atmosphere.

'True. She's a scheming old cow herself.' Then, suddenly serious, Julie Walters looks at herself in the mirror. 'In fact, Mrs Mann is really quite unpleasant.'

She's meant to be. As Alan Bleasdale says, 'Mrs Mann and Bumble may be wonderfully funny and hopelessly sex-charged all the way through, but at the end of the day they're wiped out because of what they've done. They're destitute, wrecked, destroyed and left in the Workhouse – as they were in Dickens.'

But where Alan Bleasdale has departed from Dickens, Bumble-wise, is to make his Mrs Mann an amalgam of the original Mrs Corney and Mrs Mann. In Dickens it's Mrs Corney who runs the Workhouse and Mrs Mann who has the Baby Farm. The main reason for doing this was their names. 'I know Dickens loved silly names, but I just couldn't cope with Mrs Corney.'

As Julie Walters says, 'My Mrs Mann is really very similar to Mrs Corney in the book – although Alan's added lots. The humour, for instance. I just loved doing the opening scene.' Adopting the voice of Mrs Mann as a drunken shrew, she does an action replay of banishing Sally from her birthday party. 'Another bit I *loved* doing was the fight we have. When I read about it in both the book and the script it was the funniest thing...she throws a teapot at his head and his hat comes off and, for a bit of variety, Dickens says, she gets in and scratches his face. Alan put the whole of Dickens' description [of that scene] in the script. It's *very* funny.'

It's also very indicative of the fact that Julie Walters does her homework. She may be working with old friends; she may be playing a part that involves a great amount of fun – but she's read her source-material. Not everyone who has a part specifically written for them would do that.

Then Julie is called into wardrobe. When she returns she's wearing the dress in which Mrs Mann marries Bumble. She looks down at the pristine fabric with a mock-grimace. 'It should really have a stain or two, don't you think? Little spots of gin.' Then she pats her hair. 'It changes as Mrs Mann

progresses, you know. And it gets really tight as well. When she's in the trenches it gets really close to her head – it's like a bullet in the end.' And then she's off again, revelling in Mrs Mann.

On the same day as Julie Walters was talking, her fans in the UK were revelling in a programme about her: an *Omnibus* special about her life. 'I'm glad I'm not in England tonight,' she says when asked about it. 'I'd have to go around explaining to people why their interviews had been cut. I think people who aren't in the business would be hurt by that. So I'll say well, look, Sir Peter Hall was cut...Actually,' she adds suddenly, 'I found it quite upsetting. We went over my mother's life and to her home; went on a journey I'd never done. I was quite upset when I came away. She's dead, my mother, so it kind of made me mourn her again. She was brought up in Ireland and I met neighbours who told me things about her and my grandparents.'

As she talks, all traces of Mrs Mann disappear, leaving a very pensive Julie Walters. 'My mother ran away from Ireland – it caused a huge thing – so I heard all about that. It was strange hearing all those stories. Quite therapeutic, but strange. Maybe it was a good thing. It's a shame,' she finishes in a near-whisper, 'that families are so spread out...' Then she grins. 'You know, I suddenly found out that my uncle and all sorts of relations did amateur dramatics. People had said that "no, there's no acting in your family", and then I find out that they were doing it all the time but keeping quiet about it. I suppose they thought it wasn't something you encouraged in people, that you got your showing off out of the way.' Just as one is wondering how that sort of attitude affected the ebullient Julie Walters as a girl, she giggles. 'Apparently my grandfather used to recite great court cases. He wasn't boring at all...'

A few moments later she and David Ross are called on set to celebrate their marriage. Later that day, everyone finds cause for another, real-life celebration: Julie Walters has been awarded an OBE. But there is no wild partying – it's not Julie's style. One can't *quite* imagine Mrs Mann accepting congratulations with the same self-effacing restraint.

Mrs Leeford ✦ Lindsay Duncan

Lindsay Duncan would have been unable to play Mrs Leeford but for two strikingly different (and rather unlikely) phenomena. One is Concorde. The other is a very short play by Harold Pinter.

Or rather, those are the *enabling* reasons; the mechanisms by which her presence was possible (this will make sense in a minute). There is a third factor. 'I wouldn't be here,' says Lindsay Duncan, 'without Alan's...without his...his *lunacy*.' She throws back her head and laughs. 'He's mad – but in the best possible way. He simply would *not* give up .' Alan Bleasdale admits to being demented about the whole issue, but takes no credit for the fortuitous resolution. 'That was all down to Keith Thompson,' he says. 'You have no idea what somersaults he had to perform to get Lindsay on board...'

Here's the background. Over two years ago, Alan phoned Lindsay to tell her that he'd written a part for her in *Melissa*. 'I told him I couldn't because I was committed to this Harold Pinter play – *Ashes to Ashes*. He wasn't entirely thrilled by that...' Cut to last year and another phone call – this time about the part of Mrs Leeford, again written for Lindsay. 'He said, "I've got you this time, I'm giving you so much notice." I felt sick. I had to tell him that I couldn't do it; what's worse, I had to tell him it was for the same reason: I was doing the same play – in New York. Alan said that he's never been thwarted twice in succession by someone called Harold.'

Lindsay Duncan stops to take a sip of her hot chocolate. It was supposed to be a cool gin and tonic on the terrace of a Prague bar, but that idea got rained on. Escaping from a characterless hotel sounded good in theory – but in practice was different.

As was Alan Bleasdale's theory that Lindsay would play the part of Mrs Leeford. 'It was impossible. Whichever way you looked at it, it just wasn't going to happen. Alan sulked and told me that he had no more writing in him – so I said don't give me that old bollocks. Then he put his back out and said that with any luck, although he was in pain and in a wheelchair, they'd have to delay shooting.' They didn't, and by this time Lindsay was in New York. 'But he kept phoning and telling me there *must* be a way. Well of course I started to go mad as well. I turned into a female Alan Bleasdale and

phoned Keith [Thompson], telling him that it was unimaginable that I couldn't play this part...I *had* to play this part...someone's got to imagine the unimaginable and make it happen.' Lindsay makes an expansive gesture – something that she does a lot, in contrast to the very controlled, precise manner in which she chooses her words – and finishes with, 'It was all insane really and so, to cut a long story short, it *did* happen.'

But only because Harold Pinter's play was very short, enabling Lindsay to take the night flight to England, be driven up to Cumbria, do some acting, go back to London, and then take Concorde back to New York in time for the next evening's performance. 'I did that twice in less than a week. It has to be said that it wasn't a pleasant experience. At one point I said I was going to kill Alan.'

This is all beginning to sound dangerously like a little love-in between Alan Bleasdale and his favourite actors. It's not: it's just a further illustration of the way (explained by Lindsay Duncan in Chapter One) in which Alan Bleasdale operates. And Lindsay herself is at pains to point out that 'I'm in no way painting myself as the key player. This could be related to anyone else involved...it's not that I'm important to this project.'

Wrong. Lindsay Duncan as Mrs Leeford not crucial to this project? The role is pivotal: Mrs Leeford has drunk deeply from the sour chalice of a ruined life, and she spits out the lot, infecting everyone around her. Here, she drives the plot of *Oliver Twist*.

'She is,' says Lindsay, 'the monster diva, isn't she? She sees the world entirely through her eyes. And she's the essence of cruelty – but it's believable. You have to believe that, when she was married off in her late 20s, she was this *gorgeous* creature; with all this *stuff*, all this energy and passion she could hardly keep a lid on. And then she's married to this weak *boy*. I mean, what are they going to do with each other? They can't satisfy each other – in any way. Frustrations on every level: physical, emotional, mental, intellectual – and *social*. In those days marriage for someone like her was the only way to achieve status in society. And that's what gave you power. And she never got anything – all her needs were thwarted.'

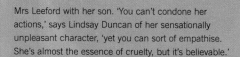

Mrs Leeford with her son. 'You can't condone her actions,' says Lindsay Duncan of her sensationally unpleasant character, 'yet you can sort of empathise. She's almost the essence of cruelty, but it's believable.'

Here is Dickens' one brief mention – using Brownlow as his mouthpiece – of the couple (Mr and Mrs Leeford) whose ill-fated marriage is pivotal to the plot of the book. '...the misery, the slow torture, the protracted anguish of that ill-assorted union. I know how listlessly and wearily each of that wretched pair dragged on their heavy chain through a world that was poisoned to them both. I know how cold formalities were succeeded by open taunts; how indifference gave place to dislike, dislike to hate, and hate to loathing...' And Monks was the fruit of that loathing.

She did, however, get a son out of it. For a moment Lindsay Duncan closes her eyes and reflects on the only thing she shares with Mrs Leeford. 'I'm the mother of a *much loved* son. When you become a mother your sense of mortality is heightened... it's like a layer of skin has been peeled away. Your perceptions change. But then her's changed too, in a different way. Unmet desires, unmet needs – and then this child who she perceives to be abnormal just becomes a dead weight she's dragging around. It all leads to her unrelenting cruelty. Her cruelty to her son is *breathtaking*.' Then Lindsay Duncan, so patently a creature of light, mulls over the magnetically black attraction of her character. 'We're all so attracted to the dark side, aren't we? And we like to have it acted out for is – it's a kind of relief in a way. Cruelty is part of the human condition. It's not something you subscribe to, but you recognise it. And Dickens' world was a very, very cruel one.'

Then, half in stupefied disgust, half in reluctant admiration, Lindsay refers to the scene where Mrs Leeford, very much down on her uppers, is 'hobbling off with this awful man to do God knows what – we call it the scene the poke in the park,' she says with a laugh. Then, more seriously, 'Her treatment to her son is breathtaking there – but she also says she's always wanted more than revenge. She wanted a gracious life.'

And that's it: the word one has been looking for to describe Lindsay Duncan. Gracious. Leaving the Prague bar and heading into the Old Town Square, she's told that the bar opposite is the English pub, where she could go for a pint of lager should she ever feel the need. If one can giggle graciously then that's what she did – before floating off into the rain.

Mr Leeford ⸱⤙⸱ Tim Dutton

The last piece of theatre that Tim Dutton acted in was Evelyn Waugh's *A Handful of Dust*, in which he played Tony Last, the character forever consigned to reading Dickens to a mad old Englishman in the Amazon rainforest. Had the play been a bit longer (by about sixty hours) he might have got round to reading *Oliver Twist* again. 'But no,' says Tim, 'I read it a long time ago. Probably at school.'

Tim did, however, remember that there was no Mr Leeford – beyond a brief mention – in Dickens' book. 'So I was intrigued when Alan Bleasdale said he's written this part for me; it really appealed to me that the father of Oliver Twist was an entirely new character. We all know Dickens' characters quite well and they all have something to stand up to. So I was really pleased to have this completely new character and all these plots and sub-plots and all these ridiculous comical moments.'

On the subject of comedy, Tim Dutton may soon be hitting our screens in what (talking of comparisons) may be the new *Cheers* – if only because the new sitcom (in which he plays the lead) is penned by the same writers. 'We've only done the pilot, but there's been great feedback so far. It's about pilgrims – as in the Mayflower settlers – and I'm the only English guy in it. Sitcoms don't normally grab me, but the writing was so good – so English.'

You can't get much more English than Mr Leeford, but he's not very funny. 'No,' admits Tim. 'There are moments, but he's basically this feckless, though decent, character. And he's absolutely ebullient in his single-mindedness. He just charges into things. If you think about it, he's basically falling in love for the first time. He's been in a very demanding and mentally abusive relationship with his wife, and now he's found love at last. He doesn't deal with it in a particularly mature way – all that rushing about. But if you haven't fallen in love before, it does something to you, and you have no point of reference. You know what you're doing is stupid but you think "I don't care – it feels great".'

Alan Bleasdale after the first time his student daughter met Tim Dutton (who performed in her graduation film): 'Apparently he charmed everyone completely, bought wine and wouldn't even take expenses. He was also stunning on video – never mind film. And by happy coincidence I was looking for a leading man for Melissa...Which just goes to show that doing good things can be very good for you.'

What Tim Dutton is doing now is waiting to be killed by Lindsay Duncan. 'I haven't worked with her before; I'm really looking forward to it. We only have that one scene together. Well, we can't have any more. I'm dead...'

He has, however, already done all his scenes with Sophia Myles (Agnes), but has yet to film the scene with Uncle Richard and the infamous goitre. 'I can't wait for that: I have to drag him out of the water by the goitre. It was fantastically funny on paper, but I wonder what it'll be like filming it.'

That scene will be filmed in Marienbad; the murdering one in Doksany; previous ones in London and Oxfordshire...if there's one thing Tim shares with Mr Leeford, it's 'all that rushing about.' 'Yes, you're flown in and next morning you're in front of the camera at 8 a.m. and you just have to bang it out. TV takes a great deal more discipline than film, you have so much more time in film. That's why it's been a joy working with Renny. It's been a real pleasure. I enjoy watching him paint pictures; I like the way he interacts with the actors. I mean the majority of us enjoy input and often on TV there isn't any. There just isn't time. Renny somehow makes time.'

If one constructs a frame of reference around Tim's words, the time factor really becomes apparent. There is one day scheduled for the Marienbad shoot – and Marienbad is two hours' drive from Prague. The Art, Camera, Sound, Electrical, Make-up, Costume, Medical and Catering departments have to be there to shoot and attend to the actors and extras (including '10 x Spa Corpulent Men, 4 x Spa Users and 6 x Spa Attendants'). Most of these people have never set foot in the place before – and Renny Rye *has* to shoot the entire scene in one day. He has absolutely no choice. Apart from the fact that the spa has only been hired for one day, the schedule demands that the entire crew then decamp to Chesky Krumlov – 175 km from Prague – the following morning.

It's no wonder that Tim Dutton, although he's loving every minute of it, is entertaining secret fantasies about 'taking a whole summer off to play cricket.' Dream on Tim.

Dickens had an inordinate fondness for silly names, some of them cringe-making to a modern audience. Yet Bumble is a triumph – more than 150 years later, we still bumble on. But there's more to this character than meets the eye. Vainglorious he may be, he's also surprised by the awakening of avuncular feelings regarding Oliver **(this page)**: feelings successfully and fatally quashed **(right)** by thoughts favouring his own advancement.

'I spend hours,' says David Ross, 'transforming myself from decrepit old sod that I am into the young and gorgeous Mr Bumble.' Then, as part of that process, he extracts his perfectly fine set of false teeth and replaces them with Mr Bumble's hideous gnashers. The effect is startling. This is the later Bumble, prior to his becoming an inmate of the Workhouse, and he hasn't aged well. He is, in fact, a decrepit old sod.

'I like to think I have a very fine collection of false teeth,' says David. 'A lot of actors won't admit to having them, but I haven't had a real tooth in my head since I was twenty, so I don't mind talking about them. They actually get me quite a lot of work: it's a luxury for a character actor like myself. In the series I'm doing after this they actually fly out into a flambé...'

These agile and versatile bits of porcelain contribute to the chameleon-like quality of David Ross. 'People are always saying there's something vaguely familiar about me, but they can't quite put their finger on it. I rather like that; they can't remember where they've seen me.' They've actually seen him all over the place: as the inspector in the recent West End production of *An Inspector Calls*; in *Vanity Fair* – and in every single Alan Bleasdale production. He's also done a stint on *Coronation Street*. In the early 90s – and with fabulously bouffant hair – he played the part of Vera Duckworth's lover Lester Fontaine.

'I love doing Bleasdale's stuff. I love Dickens as well. In fact I try to read at least one Dickens a year. I read *Oliver Twist* two years ago, again when I knew I was doing this, and now I'm completely trapped in Twist-land as it's the only book I've brought with me.' He must be something of an authority on the original Bumble now as well as the Bleasdale one. 'He's slightly better-spoken in Dickens, with a lot of eccentricities of speech

which Alan's taken out. In a way that's limiting – but stretching in another way. It means I have to find other ways to act out his eccentricities. In the scenes with Mrs Mann there's the opportunity to act the overblown aspect; to play him thinking he's such a wonderfully marvellous and authoritative human being. Of course he has to be pompous and full of himself to cover his own inadequacy. He has to cling on to power because he's desperately afraid of losing it. Same with money – that's why he marries Mrs Mann.'

This Bumble, David goes on to say, is rather more lecherous than the Dickens' one. 'Well, I'm a bit of a lech on the quiet. I like women. And I'm a bit mischievous.' Then David looks a little alarmed. 'But I'm not seedy like Bumble.' The character, however, is not all bad. 'He's a very well-rounded character – he *does* have a heart. That comes out in a couple of the scenes with Oliver.'

Bumble is, by turns, wonderfully funny, cringe-making and appalling. But it is, one suspects, a tricky part to play. The character has to progress from being, in David's words, 'a very pompous, happy, empty-headed fellow into a crushed human being'. That sort of progression is one at which David Ross excels – he's played several similar roles – although he is characteristically modest about his abilities. 'I don't know why... I just seem to be offered parts where I end up a broken man.' And broken (teeth apart) is the last word one would ever dream of applying to David; he's brimming with bonhomie.

Later that day, he is seen rushing onto set with Lucy, a highly attractive Czech member of the production crew. 'This is the sort of story you want,' he cries. 'Bumble elopes with young blonde.' Then he remembers where he's going – to play the scene where he meets his nemesis. 'Actually,' he adds with a grin, 'Bumble's off to get stung...'

Mr Bumble ·· David Ross

Monks ·•· Marc Warren

In real life this man is blond, blue-eyed, and has a captivating smile. The make-up department can only go so far in his transformation. The rest is down to something beyond artifice: astonishing skill.

'As soon as I started the audition I thought I hadn't a hope. I had no idea what I was doing, to be honest. I was faking some sort of twitch, but I didn't really have a clue. I knew the character was an epileptic, but I knew nothing about epilepsy. Renny told me not to worry, that you didn't get a part like this on the first read anyway. Afterwards, he said that as soon as I started he knew he wanted me.' Marc Warren smiles – then shrugs. 'Well, that's what he said anyway…'

And he meant it. Director Renny Rye later corroborates this, adding that 'I was 80 per cent sure that he'd be good for it the minute he put his head round the door. There was something about his face and something about the way he put his hands round the door. There was also a fantastic vulnerability that came through as soon as he started reading, but I jokingly said to the casting director that I don't think I've ever cast an actor because of his knuckles before.'

The character of Monks, by common accord, was a fantastically difficult one to imagine. There was no celluloid template to recreate (or ignore) and nor, more importantly, was there much in Dickens beyond a shadowy figure of menace, twisted and crippled by evil desires, who ends up in prison. Furthermore, there was Alan Bleasdale's intense passion and sympathy for the character. It was probably fortunate for Marc Warren that, initially, he thought he was up for a 'very minor role. I'd never heard of Monks and I hadn't read *Oliver Twist*.'

Renny Rye's intuitive reaction to Marc is all the more astonishing when one considers the differences between the character and the actor. Monks is dark and tortured: Marc is blond and – seemingly – sorted. Monks twitches even when he's not having a fit: Marc has a remarkable stillness about him. Monks is frankly frightening: Marc is friendly.

(Catch him off-set and he'll be playing frisbee with Sam Smith, teaching him card tricks, or getting ready for a night out.) Monks first appears as a 17 year-old – and then ages ten years. Marc is 32. In desperation, and mindful of Renny's words, one looks at his knuckles for clues. Nothing. They're…well, *knuckles.*

But there's something about the eyes. Marc Warren has incredibly piercing blue eyes and Monks, in Nancy's words, has 'eyes that lurk'. He also, of course, has one brown eye and one blue – director Renny Rye's idea. Very spooky. And when he's in character, Marc admits that 'people are really wary of talking to me. It's those eyes.' That apart, one suddenly realises that looking for similarities is all a piece of nonsense: why should there be any? Marc Warren is playing Monks because he's an *actor* – and a damn fine one too.

He's good at shrugging off praise as well. 'The look of Monks helps – it's just amazing and it does so much of the work for me. I just go into make-up, Lesley [the make-up designer] puts the eye in, and from then on…' Then he laughs. 'It's a total transformation for me. Lesley just embellished on my normal faults (Marc has very slight scars on the right side of his face). It's the only job I've ever done where you go into make-up for ages and end up looking worse…'

The arresting look apart, Marc really does have a challenging job to do. Far from being a minor role, Monks features prominently in *Oliver Twist*. And, of course, he also suffers from epilepsy. Portraying that condition on screen requires not just sensitivity, but accuracy. 'Alan was very keen on me doing research,' recalls Marc, 'and Kate Norbury [Alan's researcher] put me in touch with the National Society for Epilepsy.' Marc, by the way, would like to credit that Society for the help they gave him.

'They were brilliant: showed me everything they could and told me all about the different types of epilepsy. They don't just classify it as _grand mal_ and _petit mal_ any more – there are all different types of seizures. Myoclonic...partial seizures... generalised seizures. Tonic is when you stiffen up; clonic is a full-on _grand mal_; atonic is when you collapse onto the floor. We worked out that Monks had Complex Partial Epilepsy – that would tally with him being hit on the right side of his temple lobe when he was knocked over by a horse and cart.'

It's all a far cry from the role that Marc is best known for: the bent cop Douggie Raymond in _The Vice_. 'He's a right bastard – but playing him put me on the map a bit.' That map, one suspects, will have to be redrawn after this. But, again, Marc deflects any praise for his interpretation of Monks. 'It's all there in the stage directions; and you just don't normally get that any more. The script does most of the work for me. Alan Bleasdale's such a brilliant writer.' Then Marc grins. 'I'd love to work for him again. You can tell him that.'

left: Monks is the link between the good and the bad. Bill Sikes **(right)**, is just bad. And the fearsome Bullseye was, in reality, something of a wimp. He didn't like water, preferred having his tummy tickled to acting fierce – and was only actor on set who would rather have rested then acted.

Sikes ⋅- Andy Serkis

Dickens went for the jugular with Sikes. He wrote of his own creation that he was 'utterly and incurably bad', adding that he was certain there were men like him who gave not the 'faintest indication of a better nature'. Perhaps that's why critics at the time gave the character of Nancy such a drubbing: many found her devotion to him completely unconvincing.

Alan Bleasdale, on the other hand, has created a more rounded character. 'There are certain things Alan has added which open up another side,' says Andy Serkis. 'There's more to the relationship with Nancy, and there's humour. Also he's a man who can see his own fate. There's one point when he tells Nancy that you go soft in your old age and that if they went soft now they would never see their old age. It's almost as if he can see the future bearing down on him. He's not in his prime any more – and he can see it slipping away.'

So he's a nice man, then?

'No. He's domestically violent and very brutal. And I *am* playing him brutally – some of it's stomach-churning.' And, initially, it frightened Sam Smith – he was really quite scared. 'Scared of the *character*,' corrects Andy. 'It was fine when he realised he didn't have to be scared of me. We get along really well. I mean, yes, Sikes is very violent, but, like anyone else, he's just trying to survive. He isn't *likeable*, but he does have humanity.'

He also comes with an awful lot of baggage, most if it in the shape of the late Oliver Reed. Andy smiles. 'Yes. Obviously Oliver Reed gave the definitive performance and there will be similarities...but, again, Alan has given Sikes something else.' (Spookily, one of the similarities is in looks: Andy bears more than a passing resemblance to the young Oliver Reed.)

One of the things that both Alan Bleasdale and Andy Serkis have given Sikes is a very clearly defined profession. 'He's a house-breaker – and it *was* a job. I've been reading this book about house-breaking and, basically, they worked in teams of three. They would have had a kid who goes and scouts around – I think he was called the canary – and then someone else to keep a lookout, and then the house-breaker. That's why the Chertsey robbery [at Brownlow's country house] is such a big event. They were after a really big haul.'

It turns out that Andy did more than a little light background reading. He's a method actor, and immerses himself completely in the character he's playing. 'Acting for me is like an investigation into the social and psychological background of a character. It's a fact-finding mission: I want to feel what this character is all about. It's about being specific. I can't bear performances which aren't specific. But if you know the historical and political context you know that, with Sikes, he's in constant fear of being transported. If you know that, it's going to make your performance more edgy.'

Andy has had roles in two Mike Leigh films – *Career Girls* and the forthcoming *Topsy Turvy* – and they don't come more 'method' than that. 'My character in *Career Girls* was a broker, so I worked as a broker for four months. In fact I was even offered a permanent job...' (One hopes he isn't offered a permanent job as Bill Sikes...) 'In *Topsy Turvy* I played a choreographer so I practised ballet for six months.' And for Bill Sikes he read voraciously, and then invented an entire background for the character. 'His father was a navvy and built canals. A lot of them were press-ganged: particularly strong and violent men notorious for drinking and crime. Bill's mother dies of cholera when he was two and his father just moved on – leaving him. So Bill moved into pickpocketing as a tiny child, apprenticed to someone like Fagin.' (This is all eminently possible. See Chapter Two for more background information.)

Fagin and Sikes. As thick
as thieves, locked together,
yet loathing each other.
Fagin abhors violence – the
currency in which Sikes deals.

Unlike some other method actors one could mention, Andy
doesn't dribble on in ultra-luvvie speak about his approach.
'It just gives you emotional ballast; if you have it you can plug
into the character. If you know all about the environment
and the relationships, it gives you something to return to.'
So what of his relationship with Bullseye, the fearsome
Staffordshire bull terrier? 'Thankfully I really like dogs. Of
course there were two dogs – one in England and one in the
Czech Republic. It was really important to strike up a bond
with them. Bullseye is in many ways a familiar for Bill –
that relationship is the most complete he's ever had.' Then
Andy grins. 'D'you know what the English Bullseye was
actually called? Candy. Doesn't quite conjure up a ferocious
bull terrier...'

But Candy proved dandy – although liquor, as they say, is
quicker. Didn't Andy feel he had to get plastered before acting
the part of Bill Sikes? 'Well, I can't, can I? But it does help to
have a drink.' Andy grins again. 'Even if it's only one shot...'

The urge ultimately proves too much – so you rush up to Emily Woof and announce that you've found the 'l' that fell off her name. Too late, you realise that she would be perfectly entitled to respond with a smack round the head. Instead, she laughs.

Her name apart, there are four very noticeable things about Emily Woof. The first is her looks. The second is her laugh; frequent and infectious. Then there's her propensity for using words like 'weird' and 'nuts'. The fourth is the fact that, when she's playing Nancy, there is absolutely *nothing* that reminds one of Emily. Even more strange, there is nothing in either Emily or Nancy to remind one of some of this actress's previous roles: as Robert Carlyle's wife in *The Full Monty* or as the leading lady in *The Woodlanders*. She is a complete chameleon. Or, as one of her fellow cast members on *Oliver* Twist put it, 'She's a star.'

But at the moment she's not being given very starry treatment. Thanks to a startlingly disorganised interviewer, she's being forced to sit outside a grotty café under a flyover on the outskirts of Prague and she's just had a carton of UHT milk poured over her dress. 'Never mind,' she says with a giggle, 'I'll just pretend I spilled sun cream.'

She's brilliant at 'just pretending'. The previous day, she shot her biggest scene, 'the longest scene I've ever done', with Nancy revealing all to Brownlow and Co. The length of that scene would make it a challenge for any actor, but it was doubly so for Emily. Six weeks previously she filmed her arrival at Brownlow's front door: yesterday she had to continue as if it were one fluid sequence. 'I was quite nervous. I'd just flown into Prague to do that scene – that was quite weird – but I suppose it helped that Nancy was also coming into an environment that was completely new to her. I could have just sat there like a frozen stick, but...well, I hope I'm getting it...' Then, unconsciously, she puts her hand to her mouth and, Nancy-like, seems to shrink into herself. Cue to ask her how she gets into character.

left: Emily Woof as Nancy and **above,** Zuzana Krausova as the young Nancy. The latter only appears once – and fleetingly – so it wouldn't have mattered if she barely resembled Emily Woof. That she looks almost identical was pure joyous chance.

'Oh,' Emily seems a little non-plussed. 'I don't even think about it. It's just what happens. 'My main thing was, God, what an honour to even think of playing Nancy. It's one of the great pathetic – in the real sense of the word – roles to play. Especially in this script. I really like the fact that she's not like the Nancy in the musical. She's drunk and bedraggled a lot; always in a bit of a state. And it's a real pleasure to speak her lines. The script's very shiny. It's very clear for me what to play.' Then she looks suddenly doubtful. 'It's difficult to gauge how "big" to play her – that's why I was a bit nervous about yesterday's performance – I wasn't sure how big or small to be.' Everyone on set thought she gauged it perfectly, but her words provide a good indication of the fragmented nature of acting. We, the viewers, feel familiar with Nancy by the time she plays what is nearly her last scene, but for the actress herself it was one of the first.

As an actress Emily Woof is all the more remarkable for the fact that she never attended drama school. 'I used to write and put on shows for myself. You know, just go out and do them.' As if this were the most normal thing in the world, she then continues with 'I was also a trapeze artist, so I incorporated that into my shows. I'd do stuff at Fringe shows, the Edinburgh Festival and international shows. I never even thought of film... but it suddenly happened.' Anything else? 'Oh yes, I still write. I've written a screenplay so I'm kind of all over the place because I've just come back from Cannes. It was weird; nuts. They're on the phone all the way through screenings. My film's now been optioned so I'm looking for a producer.' Then she pauses and reflects for a moment. 'I do think your acting muscles get slightly slack if you haven't appeared in front of a camera for a while.' Suddenly she lets out a great peal of laughter. 'Actually, it's only two weeks since I was in front of the camera: I don't know what I'm talking about, do I?'

Oh, but we think she does.

'My recollection of Grimwig is of a jolly character prone to getting grumpy – all this "I'll eat my head" business. I think this adaptation makes him slightly darker and more cynical,' says John Grillo. 'Like when he says to Brownlow that "I've told you before this is what comes of being good. No good ever comes of it." It's a small part,' he adds in his carefully measured tones, 'but I find it interesting and rewarding.'

This becomes more than evident as John Grillo continues to talk about Grimwig, Dickens, and Alan Bleasdale's adaptation. Phrases like 'spiritual redemption', 'emotional momentum' and 'the underlying truth of the story' trip off his tongue as he discusses a subject about which he quite clearly knows much. But as he talks, one is reminded of a different adaptation – nothing to do with Dickens. Then it clicks. John Grillo played the pompous, unctuous Mr Samgrass – Sebastian Flyte's tutor/companion – in the legendary adaptation of *Brideshead Revisited*. It comes as quite a surprise to realise that, for if there was one trait that Mr Samgrass quite conspicuously lacked it was charm. And John Grillo has it in spades.

As the name suggests, Grimwig was something of a caricature in Dickens' *Oliver Twist*. Here he's slightly darker and with a definite cynicism – more of a real person. Furthermore, his relationship with Brownlow was static in the original. Here it changes and, ultimately, flounders.

He grins at the mention of *Brideshead*. Revisiting (sorry, couldn't help that) something so far in the past is rather like saying 'Oh didn't you used to be...?' but John doesn't take umbrage. People still hark back to the nostalgia of *Brideshead*, and the fact that in those days they had the money to make programmes in a leisurely fashion. 'Actually,' contradicts John, 'it wasn't particularly leisurely. I'd come from doing a lot of theatre and very little TV, and it came as a shock to me that we barely rehearsed. We hardly even talked about what we were doing. It came as a surprise to me that it came out so ravishingly well.'

John's professional palate is now huge and multi-layered. A writer as well as a veteran of radio, TV and theatre drama and comedy, he concurs with pretty well every fellow thespian that comedy is the hardest thing to do. 'Which is why Alan's interpretation of Grimwig is so good. It's not exaggerated. The name Grimwig – and that catchphrase of "I'll eat my head" – is enough. I'm trying to approach him in the same way as everyone else is playing their parts – more restrained than exaggerated.' At that moment he's called back onto set and, after very little rehearsal, gives a performance that goes down ravishingly well.

Mr Grimwig •• John Grillo

Agnes Fleming ∙▸∙ Sophia Myles

'Apparently I've got a period face, so I always get thrown into a corset. They're hell, actually. It's like wearing a metal toilet-roll round your waist.' Sophia Myles giggles. 'But there's nothing else I'd rather do than this. These have been the best two months of my life – even though I really didn't know what I was letting myself in for.'

Sophia had actually let herself in for a day being harnessed to the top of a cliff, followed by a good couple of weeks' worth of rain, wind, mud and ditches. Basically, she got anything the elements (real or special effected) could throw at her. And then she had to cry. A lot. 'Someone told me that crying is one of your body's devices for making you tired: a mechanism for forcing you to sleep it off. But I couldn't: I couldn't stop crying when I came off set, and I had to cry every day for about two weeks. It was physically so taxing.'

Sophia Myles doesn't look like the crying type. 'No, I'm not usually. I'm not particularly emotional. But when I read the script I burst into tears – and that is just not me. It's Agnes: the part is just the epitome of tragedy. I mean every time you think it can't get any worse for her she's hit over the head with a sledgehammer. It's just so sad.'

Interestingly, Sophia was wandering round the stage set at Barrandov the previous day when Agnes' birthing-room was pointed out to her. Workmen were adding the final touches in the shape of damp, cracks and the odd bit of mould. Sophia immediately stiffened when she saw the dismal little room where Agnes would meet her death. 'Oh the poor girl,' she whispered. Despite the fact that she knew she would have to spend the best part of a day giving birth there (the sequence is seen on two separate occasions and has two versions), her reaction was for Agnes, not herself.

Acting was never an ambition for Sophia Myles. 'I fell into it – and now it's all I want to do. But it's scary...it's disturbing that this is now my dream. They say that two of the worst things that can happen to you in life are not achieving your dreams, and achieving your dreams. I'm here now – but what happens next?'

If what's happened in the past is anything to go by, Sophia doesn't have much to worry about. She started acting because drama was one of her options for GCSE and, she says with a grin, 'I thought it would be the easiest. I was a Cockney slapper in this play we did. A director from the BBC saw it, asked me to do an audition and the next thing I knew I was playing Lady Jane Grey in *The Prince and The Pauper*.' Then, whilst she was doing her A Levels, came Fay Weldon's *Big Women*, a spell at the Birmingham Rep and *Mansfield Park*. 'Lindsay Duncan was my mother in that. And Sam Smith was my brother. It's funny, isn't it? Now I'm Sam's mother and Lindsay's enemy...'

Sophia was accepted at Cambridge to study philosophy, but has deferred it to continue acting. 'I *will* go,' she says, 'but it's so stimulating to learn from other sources as well. And you learn a lot from being on a film set. I mean you're surrounded by all these people; they become your mates; they see you at your worst and your best...it's like being married to them all. But film sets are also very lonely places; you live in hotels all the time and you're actually on your own a lot. What you have to remember,' she concludes, 'is that it's not real. It's pretend.'

But even when she was pretending to play Agnes, her distress was often real. 'I know,' she says. Then she grins. 'I remember saying to Renny, "this Tim Dutton better be nice. After all this I deserve something good".' She got it. Tim, she says, is 'fantastic'.

Agnes; the epitome of tragedy. 'To be honest,' says Sophia Myles, 'I used to think it was a load of drivel when people said they find it difficult to get out of character when they come off stage – but I couldn't stop crying for the first two weeks.'

I haven't done much since [Rosamunde Pilcher's] *Coming Home* – just a bit of radio and a reshoot on something and a small part in *Star Wars* – so when I got this I was thinking "Thank God. Finally!"'

Keira Knightley is fourteen. When you're told this you just gawp in an open-mouthed, dead-fish sort of way. It just doesn't seem possible. She looks, at the very least, seventeen. But it's not only that startlingly beautiful face that belies her age: it's her voice, her mannerisms and the way she handles herself. And her attitude towards her career.

The words 'precocious' and 'pushy parent' have already sprung to mind, and been dismissed. Keira appears totally unaffected by the strange world in which she spends as much of her life as she can. And her mother, playwright Sharman Macdonald – here as her chaperone – is still slightly ambivalent about the whole thing. But children don't just fall into acting by accident – someone, surely, must have pushed her? Sharman grins. 'You'd better ask Keira.'

'Oh they *really* didn't want me to do this,' says her daughter. (Sharman, for the record, has retired out of earshot to read a book.) 'They're both in the business themselves. (Keira's father is the actor Will Knightley.) But you see I've wanted to do this since I was three.' *Three?* 'Yes. You know how girls go through this princess phase...but I thought, "No, I don't want to be a princess, I want to *pretend* to be a princess."' Keira bursts out laughing. Then she adds that she was 'really trailing at school when I was six. They couldn't get me to work. I kept badgering them about getting an agent, so they finally said I could get photos done [to present to an agent] if I worked every day through the summer holidays. They *really* didn't think I would

'I never wear pink. They phoned me up and asked if there's any colour I don't wear and I thought, well, they probably won't give me pink so I'll keep quiet. And what happens? Every single dress Rose wears is pink. I feel like I'm trapped in this pink meringue...But, no, they're very pretty.'

do it – but I did.' She carried on working – and bludgeoned her parents into getting her an agent. Seven years down the line, she reckons 'they're beginning to come round to it.'

But Keira, had she been listening to her parents when she was an embryo, would have realised that she would be born into the business – literally. 'My husband bet me a script for another baby,' says Sharman later. Eh? 'Well, I wanted another baby [Keira has a 20-year-old brother] but we were quite poor so my husband said that if I sold the script I was writing we could have one.' Then she laughs. 'I did sell it – for £2,000. We bought a car with half of it and the rest was supposed to keep us for the rest of our lives.' The play, *When I Was A Girl I Used To Scream And Shout*, was premièred at London's Bush Theatre at the same time as Keira arrived; and Keira became known as the Bush Baby.

A baby who's grown up an awful lot. And now, at the tender age of fourteen, she's filming her first love scenes. Until *Oliver Twist*, she's had a body double for anything even approaching intimacy – now she's getting married. Keira starts to giggle. out laughing. 'I know. I was a bit worried about the kissing but it was fine...very nice and innocent. But I've been put off marriage for ever. It was my first scene with David [Bark-Jones] and we had to walk down the aisle about 24 million times. Bizarre. I thought, No, I don't want to do that again...'

Anyway, she can't. At least not for a while. She has to go back to school.

Rose Fleming ⇢ Keira Knightly

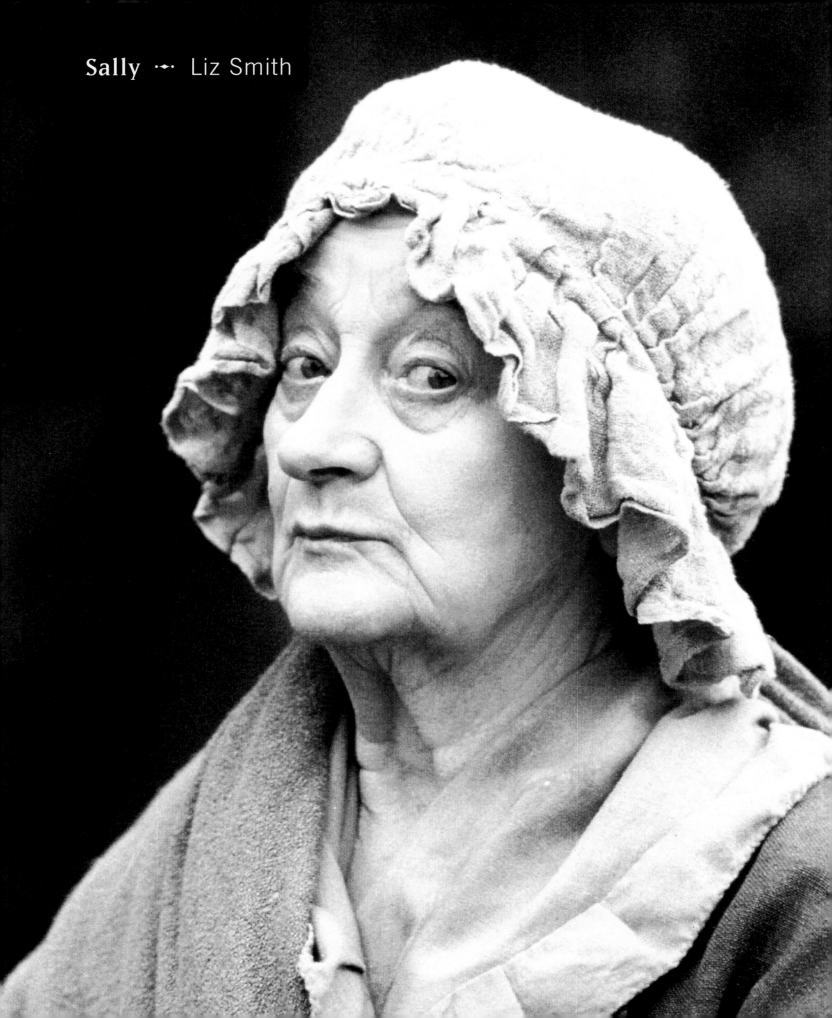

Sally ⋅⋅ Liz Smith

One of Britain's best-loved character actresses is reeling off her string of credits. 'I've been a postman, a filing clerk, I've worked in every shop in the West End, I've been in a factory inspecting bags...oh, God knows...really slogging jobs. Miserable jobs, long hours and years of grinding poverty. You see, I had these two small children to bring up on my own.' Then she begins to look concerned. 'Do I have a bit of crisp on my lip?'

No. There is no crisp. But there is something in her manner, as she asks the question, that reminds one of the characters she plays on screen. Her BAFTA-winning performance as Maggie Smith's mother in *A Private Function*; her role in *The Vicar of Dibley*; Caroline Aherne's grandmother in *The Royle Family*, and countless others. Liz Smith may not have been a 'name' for very long, but she's been acting all her life. 'I started when I was eight or nine. I was living all alone with my granny and she sent me out to mix with other children. We did these little plays in church halls and I was doing exactly the same thing as I'm doing now – being silly. But I loved it. I got all this warmth from the audience and I thought, I want to do this.'

So she did it. For year after year Liz Smith slogged away at every job under the sun, raised two children on her own, and acted when she got the chance. 'And I can't tell you how often I didn't get a chance. I couldn't get an agent – they wouldn't have me – so I was thrown out of every office. But I knew I would get a chance. I knew there was some sort of little excitement between me and the audience. I *had* to get a chance.'

Liz Smith is rather matter-of-fact about all this. But her audience (this time, of one) is reeling. And rather humbled. This isn't some Hollywood bimbo wittering on about a couple of years of waitressing before her 'big break': this is an elderly lady talking of very nearly *half a century* of single-minded determination. And the odds were really stacked against her. She's coy about the shadows in her life, but several of them flit by as she talks: 'I was left without parents when I was two'; 'my husband left when the children were tiny'; 'oh yes, terrible poverty' and 'a lot of us crawl into this job for security'. Yet there isn't a single ounce of self-pity attached to these snippets of Liz Smith's life. She's simply recounting the things she had to do, and that thing she always wanted to do. Act. 'It was all I had to hang on to.'

She clung in there through years of Rep, Unity Theatre and then 'Charles Marovitz happened next. He was the great method director who came from New York in the mid 20s. He brought the Stanislavsky approach to this country and I worked for him for five years. He didn't pay a penny I might add – so now you know about the postman jobs. Then he got a chance to go to the RSC with Peter Brook to do the famous *King Lear* and just dropped us. Can you imagine? Five years of improvisation, and that was it. Finished.'

But it didn't finish Liz Smith. She joined the Butlin's Rep Company and worked there every summer for years until her children were grown up. 'By that time I was middle-aged and it was then I heard about a young director who was making his first feature and had cast the young people but not the old ones. He wanted someone who'd done improvisation. I got the part.' And here was her chance. The young director was the now-legendary Mike Leigh. 'He'll be my hero for ever. Nobody else would pick me up off the floor.'

She's risen to great heights since then – always playing 'old' and usually being silly. 'I've worked in Prague before, you know. I was a "strange attendant" in *The Young Indiana Jones*. That's me – strange and gin-sodden. I'm very gin-sodden here. My liver's packed up. I think there was a lot of consolation in drink in those days.' Liz takes a pensive sip of her drink – coffee. A complete failure in the method-drinking department, then.

'But I'm loving being in this. I've done Dickens before, but just the *look* of this one...the faces and the wardrobe. Each one has the stamp of a Dickens' character. Each one. And I've worked with Renny before. He's delightful to work with, he gives every little mood and expression its own rightful weight.' And if anyone should know about these things, it's Liz Smith.

Later, she's asked if she'll ever call it a day and put her feet up. 'Oh no, I'll carry on as long as they'll have me. I get worn out when I'm doing nothing. As long as someone doesn't flog me to death I'm fine.' Then she pauses. 'That did nearly happen once. I was this pirate lady in a children's TV programme and I had to hold a real sword between my teeth for nineteen takes. I lost a tooth. *That's* what I call hard.' Then, with an airy reference to developing rheumatism after being 'knocked about a bit in my career', she says that she's off to Marienbad the following day. 'I'm a spa person. I love them.' The discussion turns to Marienbad, the famous film, and the treatments on offer at the spa. Several people on the production have been wanting to go – and have seen a list of those treatments on offer. 'Have you *seen* the one at the bottom of the list?' asks Liz with a glint in her eye.

Yes. It's the one that makes colonic irritation sound as tame as flossing your teeth. Liz giggles. 'I think I'll find out about that. I might even have one...'

She probably will. The word 'game' would do Liz Smith an injustice. She's still grabbing everything life has to offer, and now she's writing about it. 'There's a lot I haven't told you about my life,' she finishes. 'I'm saving it for the book.' And what a book that promises to be.

Oliver ⸱⸱⸱ Sam Smith

An extract from the essay Sam Smith wrote about his time playing Oliver:

> *I have been beaten, whacked by Mrs Mann, thwacked with a cane, a bucket of water thrown on me and I have been shot with a real gun! The whack by Mrs Mann was not hard, the cane was rubber and I had padding in my trousers, the water from the bucket was warm and there was only gunpowder in the gun; it shows that all these things are special effects. Everyone in the cast are really friendly to me…but poor Oliver!!!*

It's good stuff by a nine-year-old. It's even better when you read between the lines. Sam Smith has learned a lesson that many adult actors have mysteriously failed to grasp: don't whinge. For the reality is that playing the part of Oliver Twist isn't all fun and exclamation marks. It's demanding for a child and, at times, a hard slog.

'Altogether, says Sam, '*Oliver Twist* is just great. Sometimes I wish it would never end. I've got three-and-a-half weeks left and that's just *nothing* – I want to do *way* more. But, he admits as he leans closer, 'I didn't really enjoy it after the first few weeks. You see, they did the best bits first – I mean the worst bits first.' An eloquent shudder and then, 'Oh...the first day I had that bucket of water thrown all over me and yes, it was warm, but I had to stay in these soaking clothes for the next two hours. Then they got into the good stuff: being chased by a crowd. That was really cool.' All enthusiasm again, Sam then reels off a list of highlights, punctuated with the odd bad moment. 'Of course,' he finishes in a different, entirely adult vein, 'with every film you have your ups and downs, which I've been having. Maybe it's because I'm not used to it.'

He's doing himself something of a disservice. He's got used to 'it' remarkably quickly and is completely unfazed about the enormity of the role of Oliver. One of the greatest pleasures, it seems, is that 'this is the only time I've had a name. In *Mutability* I was "child" and in *Mansfield Park* I was "Fanny Price's brother". And there, in one sentence, is Sam's CV: two tiny parts and then a leap into the big league. And, no doubt, the limelight.

But for the moment Sam is just someone else on a film set, discussing the things he misses, the things he loves and the things he's learned. 'There's loads and loads of things I never knew about. I never knew about exactly how the camera works. I've been looking closely at how it works and I've found out lots of stuff about it...' Sam proceeds to share the fruits of his discoveries – and they're all accurate.

Sam Smith is not daft. Even though he has missed nearly two months of formal schooling (he's tutored on set), he hasn't fallen behind. Half way through shooting he returned to England to sit exams, and passed them all with flying colours – a source of relief to his father who has been chaperoning Sam throughout the shoot. By law, a minor has to be made a ward of court and chaperoned whilst working abroad, and it's not always easy. Both parties are living in an unreal world, with none of the back-up they're both accustomed to. 'We're now like an old married couple,' laughs Alan Smith when he's asked about it. 'We drive each other mad.'

But who drove Sam into acting? 'No-one,' says Sam. 'My parents are absolutely not stage parents. [Nor are they present at this interview.] I had to force my Mum and Dad into even *phoning* the agent's number.' Sam looks both amused and indignant here; on the cusp, perhaps, of an 'it's not fair'. Then you remember that Sam doesn't whinge. 'I have a friend who's an actor and I went behind stage on one of his plays, which was really brilliant, and the chaperone of a little boy gave me a number for this agency. That's how it started.'

There's a strong personality behind the slight creature that is Sam Smith. A sensible and likeable one as well. When he's not acting, he may be messing about with Andy Serkis or cooing over Andy's baby – 'she's *really* sweet' – or being teased by Steve the camera operator. Alternatively, he may have his face buried in a book, be writing a story (he has an extraordinarily fertile imagination), or be asking someone the sort of question that makes adults want to grow up: as in 'if a tree falls over and there's nobody to hear it, does it actually make a sound?'

If that makes one think that Sam Smith may be too good to be true – think again. Someone not entirely unrelated to this book gave him another thorough drenching on the river at Chesky Krumlov. Sam exacted his revenge. In spades.

Inevitably, Sam Smith will be compared to Mark Lester (Oliver in the musical) and John Howard Davies (in the 40s David Lean film). By some astonishing coincidence, Sam goes to the same school that the latter attended more than fifty years ago. 'My headmaster found a letter from his father, asking for time off to play Oliver.'

Nowadays, permission for time off is still given at the discretion of the school, but the law dictates that children under fourteen can only work for forty days a year. Things were rather different in Dickens' day...

Actions speaking louder than words. Keira and Sam's off-screen relationship mirrored that of the script – with added and unfettered *joie de vivre*.

Guides to the Episodes

Wherein it is (Hopefully) Shewn How the Entire Saga
of Oliver Twist Can be Distilled Into a Few Pages

Earnest but feckless, Leeford (Tim Dutton) assures his lover Agnes (Sophia Myles) that he will return to her. Neither of them yet know that Agnes is carrying their child – and no previous adaptation of *Oliver Twist* has explored the 'back story' that Dickens tacked on at the end of the book. In Dickens, these characters exist in name only, and so does the character on the next page, the lady who provides Leeford with a very good reason for not returning from Rome...

Episode One

*Wherein it is shewn how Oliver Twist came to
be born in such sad circumstances*

It is 1826. Agnes Fleming, heavily pregnant and deeply
distraught, is standing on the top of a cliff, clutching a locket.
She's obviously contemplating suicide but, in the end, fails
to throw either herself or the locket off the cliff. She stumbles
back from the edge and struggles in pelting rain towards a
nearby town. It's grim – and it gets worse. Now in premature
labour, she is taken by some townsfolk to the workhouse where
she dies in childbirth.

Now we find out how she got herself into this grisly
predicament. Cutting to a scene months earlier, we see Agnes
with her lover, Edwin Leeford. Their affair is unknown to
Agnes' father, who is a great chum of Leeford's. Leeford,
it transpires, used to have a wife. Fleming advises him to get
another. Leeford appears rather feckless and we're not sure
that he loves Agnes until, in Dublin for four months, he buys
a locket and a ring and has miniatures of himself and Agnes
painted inside the former.

When he returns to England he finds two letters waiting for
him and, rather more alarming, a pregnant Agnes. He tells
Agnes he can't marry her because his wife, whom he married
at seventeen, is still alive. One of the letters, sent from Paris is,
in fact, from her. She's demanding more money for herself
and their son Edward. (We get the strong impression that
there is no love lost between Leeford and his wife.) The other
letter is from his uncle Richard in Rome, who is dying and
wishes to leave him everything to compensate for 'times past'.

Leeford dashes off to Rome, telling Agnes that he'll come back
and take care of everything. Before he goes, he gives her
the locket he bought in Dublin. And he drops in on his friend
Brownlow, who was best man at the wedding into which, we
now gather, he and the ailing Uncle Richard forced Leeford.
Leeford begs Brownlow to look after Agnes and the child
should anything go wrong on the journey. A further
connection between the two men is shown by a portrait of
Leeford's late sister Katherine on Brownlow's wall. She was,
we assume, Brownlow's fiancée.

As Leeford leaves London, he passes through a square where
various strolling exhibitionists are strutting their stuff.
Amongst them are Fagin, The Artful Dodger and Bill Sikes.

Mrs Leeford (Lindsay Duncan) in all her magnificent, malignant glory. Today's monster divas have Big Hair, yesterday's had Big Hats – and Mrs Leeford's are always big and bold. Her look is a composite one; costume designer Ros Ebbutt had images of Borgias and Medicis in her mind, as well Ingres portraits of fashionable and highly formidable women.

Cut to Paris, where we meet the mysterious Mrs Elizabeth Leeford and her son Edward, known as Monks. She is elegant, regal, well-preserved (she's older than Leeford), and sweeps rather than walks. Monks, on the other hand, is dark, brooding, cowed and, we suspect, not well. His mother treats him with disdain and addresses him 'with the casual expertise of true cruelty' (Alan Bleasdale). Mrs Leeford is brandishing a letter from her husband, containing the news of Uncle Richard and the prospect of more money. Money, we gather, is an extremely important commodity as far as she is concerned, and she's not going to pass up the chance of inheriting part of Uncle Richard's estate. To this end, she resolves to go to Rome herself and to tackle her estranged husband face to face.

In Rome, Uncle Richard dies almost as soon as Leeford arrives. On the advice of his Scottish lawyer, the now wealthy Leeford makes a will, providing a generous allowance for his wife and son – and including a mysterious 'safeguard' in the event of his having another son.

Back in his Rome apartment, Leeford is writing to his 'dearest darling Agnes' (presumably with the news that all soon will be well), when he is ambushed by his wife and son. The true nature of their relationship is revealed when Leeford declares that 'Dictionaries should contain your name and particulars, Elizabeth. Definition of "evil" – just your name and a brief description. "Malignancy" – your name again. "Cruelty" – see "evil" – see "malignancy" – see "Elizabeth Leeford".'

This definition turns out to be amazingly precise: Elizabeth has poured prussic acid into his wine. Then she burns his will. In his death throes, Leeford tries to attack her but, as well as being evil, cruel and malignant, she's also handy with a fruit knife and stabs him. Yet he parries her death blow with an equally fatal verbal one. His last words – and the key to all Elizabeth's subsequent actions – are 'the lawyer has a copy'.

But this lady is nothing if not resourceful. Once her anger subsides, she pockets Leeford's letter to Agnes (who is the major beneficiary of the will) and resolves to find her before the lawyer does. We are left in no doubt that 'find', in Elizabeth – speak, equates 'murder'. And, as she and Monks career away in a carriage, she begins to look on the bright side of the murder she has just committed: 'At least it will look like a proper murder now. Not by poison. Not a woman's murder.'

The true horror of all of this is its effect on Monks. He has just witnessed the murder of the father he never knew by the mother who despises him. The wretchedness of his life is becoming more and more apparent, and so are the hints that he has some sort of physical problem as well as dreadful mental scars.

Back in England, Agnes' father has discovered she is pregnant (but not by whom) and has taken her and her younger sister Rose to live away from prying eyes in the country. But there's no hiding from Mrs Leeford: she's on horseback, watching them from a nearby hill – and nominates the hapless Monks to launch a midnight attack.

The news from Rome reaches Brownlow and his lawyer, Mr Grimwig, and they duly inform Agnes' father of Leeford's murder. His distress is as nothing compared to that of Agnes – and her agony is compounded by the fact that she still cannot tell her father that Leeford was her lover. She has only shared that news with her younger sister Rose.

That night Agnes packs a bag and writes a farewell note to her father. We're not yet sure if she's planning suicide or simply running away to spare her family shame but, for the moment, she succeeds in doing neither. She is attacked by Monks. His bid to kill her fails – he falls on her, overcome by an epileptic fit. Now his earlier twitching is explained, and with it a previous conversation with his mother about a childhood accident that made him 'the way I am'. The way he is at this precise moment is severely traumatised: by his fit; by his mother's treatment; by her murdering the father who never wanted him; and by the fact that his father loved Agnes. In a macabre travesty of a loving embrace, he lies on Agnes and whispers that Leeford sent him to kill her: 'Oh yes, he didn't want you either!'

It's an unwritten rule in costume dramas that tragic heroines have to pick flowers.

Agnes' screams rouse her father and sister. She flees from Monks and from the cottage, hurtling wildly into the night. Rose runs into her bedroom and encounters Monks wielding his knife. She's terrified: even more so when, trying to scare her away, he yells that 'I am the devil! I am the bogeyman.' Monks then escapes back to his mother and confesses that his assassination attempt failed because he had a fit. Mrs Leeford is livid.

Rose and her father mount a search for Agnes, but fail to find her. Rose tells him that Leeford was the father of the unborn child. They never do find Agnes. The next day, in the Workhouse, the baby is born and Agnes dies. Even in death, she cannot escape indignity. Sally, the gin-sodden Workhouse crone, steals the locket – the only clue to Agnes's identity – from her clenched fist.

Over copious amounts of gin, the Parish Beadle, Mr Bumble, together with the Workhouse matron Mrs Mann, chooses a name for the baby: Oliver Twist.

Episode Two

In which Oliver meets new friends while others stay darkly in the background

A glimpse of Workhouse child-rearing methods: 'He won't take the gruel,' says Mrs Mann of the infant Oliver, 'and the gin isn't working.' The prognosis is not good.

Nor is it good for Agnes' father. Distraught at her disappearance, he's losing his mind. Then, after a fall from his horse, he loses his life. Rose, his only remaining child, is adopted by Brownlow. (His Leeford connection makes him feel responsible for her.)

He feels absolutely no responsibility, however, for Mrs Leeford. She storms into his house – 'her clothes constitute 1826 power dressing' – and harangues him about her late husband's will. We learn that 'he created the most ridiculous clauses and caveats if that child was born a boy'. We also discover that Brownlow, as executor of the will, is going to continue to search for Agnes and her child until that child turns twenty-one. Mrs Leeford is beside herself with rage; a rage that intensifies when she learns that if she contests the will, she and Monks stand to lose the £600 a year they've been given. Monks, who is with her, nearly has a fit (literally) when he sees Rose in Brownlow's house. Desperate to get out of the place before she sees him, he agrees to the terms of the will.

left: 'Please sir, can I have some more?' This was something of a nightmare to film as Mr Slout, Master of the Workhouse to whom Oliver (Sam Smith) addressed his question, was a Czech extra who didn't speak English. Although Vera the translator was on hand, he misunderstood her and thought that 'more' meant Oliver was going to say more so he waited for him to speak again. On all eight takes of the shot...

above right: The interior of the Baby Farm. The pot-belly stove in the corner is something of a moveable feast. The production only had one, so it doubles as itself in all sorts of locations. There were, however, 12 (real) babies in the farm, and they did what babies do. As soon as one cried, the rest followed suit...

The likelihood of Oliver even reaching the age of one, however, is diminishing by the minute. Mrs Mann and Mr Bumble pack him off to a Baby Farm – an establishment for infant to ten-year-olds. That, in theory, is the age-range. Most of the inmates die as babies...but not Oliver Twist. On his tenth birthday, Mr Bumble is obliged to return for him and take him back to the Workhouse. 'Well!', says Mrs Mann. 'You've outlived all expectations, Oliver, and by ten years.'

Cock-a-hoop about the new Poor Law Amendment Act, designed to prevent Workhouses from being places of 'all play and no work' (as if...), the Workhouse Board resolves to teach Oliver a useful trade, and set him to picking oakum at six o'clock the following morning. In the boys' dormitory that evening, discussions about demands to increase their gruel rations result in Oliver drawing the short straw and, at supper, he utters the immortal words, 'Please sir... I want some more.'

After the resultant pandemonium, Oliver is placed in solitary confinement, flogged in front of the other boys and then a notice is put on the Workhouse gates offering him for £5. Miffed that there are no takers, the Board ponders on how to lose him at sea. Happily for them, they're saved from manufacturing that predicament by an offer from Mr Sowerberry, the parochial undertaker. Mr Bumble is surprised – and deeply embarrassed – by the fact that Oliver starts crying when the time comes to leave.

There are no open arms to greet Oliver at the funeral parlour.

Mrs Sowerberry who, according to Alan Bleasdale, was 'soured by life a long time ago, perhaps at birth', is aghast at how small he is, declares him useless and shoves him into the cellar. She instructs Charlotte, her vacant and voluptuous servant, to feed him the dog's scraps. Later, Oliver is taken to a squalid apartment where a woman has died of starvation because her husband, who was begging food for her, has been sent to jail. Unlike his wife, Sowerberry takes a shine to Oliver and appoints him as a mute, clad in black, to lead the children's funeral processions. The older apprentice, Noah Claypole, is livid at being bypassed and insults Oliver's mother. Showing his mettle, Oliver wallops him with a frying pan and ends up locked in the cellar again, determined now to run away to London.

Meanwhile Monks, ten years older than when we last saw him, has realised that the annual pension left to him and his mother isn't enough. He resolves to disinherit Oliver – but first he must find him. All he has to go by is his father's letter to Agnes. He meets Fagin, now a well-known London fence, in a particularly malodorous drinking den called The Three Cripples. Fagin advises him to go to the town where Agnes went missing and to search the records for an illegitimate child born in the Workhouse. If the child is found, leers Fagin, 'I'll educate him. As we agreed. At the price we agreed.'

Later, Monks' search takes him to the funeral parlour, where he learns that the Workhouse apprentice, fitting the bill and named Oliver Twist, is in the cellar. Just as he's about to get his hands on his hated yet unknown half-brother, he has a fit and is rendered *hors de combat*.

Oliver manages to escape to London and Monks reports the fact back to Fagin at The Three Cripples. But Fagin has a trick or two up his sleeve. Now knowing Oliver's name and what he looks like, he alerts his band of pickpockets and one of them – The Artful Dodger – picks Oliver up and takes him to Fagin's den.

left: Sowerberry (Roger Lloyd Pack) and Mr Bumble attend the funeral of the pauper who died of starvation. According to an 1844 report, parish regulations called for the minimum of formalities to be observed on the death of a pauper, specifying only that a register be kept in which were recorded details about the age, sex, rank or profession of the deceased, and the cause of death.

above: Monks (Marc Warren) arrives at the seaside town to begin his search for Oliver.

Episode Three

*Containing fresh discoveries, and shewing that surprises,
like misfortunes, seldom come alone.*

Oliver is stunned and thrilled by the mesmerising magic tricks
of Fagin and the speed of the boys' hands as they produce
handkerchiefs from nowhere and the contents of his pockets
from... well, his pockets. 'How did you know it was going to be
me?' he asks Fagin, after the magician says 'Welcome, Oliver
Twist.' He's not quite sure what's going on but, especially after
meeting Nancy, he likes being there.

Even the viewer doesn't yet know as much about Oliver as
Fagin does. Monks has explained to him the 'ridiculous
clauses and caveats if the child were born a boy': if the boy is
disgraced or convicted of a crime before he comes of age, he
will be disinherited.

Cut to Mrs Mann and Mr Bumble. The former has been
widowed – a state to which we strongly suspect she has been
secretly aspiring. She takes Bumble on a wistful tour of her
sitting and bed-rooms – both crammed with glittering objects
of dubious taste from the far-flung travels of the late Captain
Mann. Bumble is enchanted; partly by Mrs Mann's heaving
bosom but mainly by her possessions, and makes a clumsy pass.
Mrs Mann feigns outrage but is interrupted by the inconvenient
news that Sally, the Workhouse crone, is dying. Sne mounts
something of a reluctant vigil. 'I can't wait much longer. I'm in

Back in London, Monks tells Fagin that he developed epilepsy
by being run down by a coach when he was four. He also
tells him that he'll give him £600 if he ensures that Oliver is
disgraced in front of Brownlow. Fagin duly plots the boy's
downfall. Dimly aware that something's up, Oliver nevertheless
accompanies Charley Bates and The Artful Dodger on a
job. Charley and Artful pick Brownlow's pockets and leave
Oliver red-faced and red-handed - holding the evidence.

Later, in The Three Cripples, Fagin tells Monks that Oliver
has been shamed and is currently at Clerkenwell Magistrates'
Court. Monks, however, says he can't pay Fagin yet as he needs
proof of Oliver's identity. Fagin tells him to get that proof or
else Brownlow will be informed of exactly who was behind the
pickpocketing scam.

Things turn sour when Charley returns with the information
that Oliver has been acquitted (a bookseller witnessed the
pickpocketing and vouched for Oliver's innocence) and,
infinitely worse, that Brownlow is a philanthropist and has
taken Oliver home with him. Fagin is incandescent with rage
and lashes out at Monks for not informing them that Brownlow
is a do-gooder. It's now vital to get Oliver back before he
informs Brownlow about his little sojourn at Fagin's den.
Nancy, who has befriended Oliver, is nominated (i.e. bullied)

After a ten-year gap, we meet Mrs Leeford again. She's living in reduced circumstances in a genteel apartment in London. Wheezing, arthritic, over made-up and not wearing well, she herself is reduced – but only in body. Her spirit (most of it gin) is still there. She thinks it's a sweet irony that Oliver is at Brownlow's. Still under the impression that he has been disgraced, she's determined to get hold of the locket to prove that the disgraced boy is indeed Oliver.

Oliver is in heaven at Brownlow's house. Fed, watered and looked after by Mrs Bedwin, he tells Brownlow that he 'never, never' will give him cause to throw him out. But Mr Grimwig, dropping in for tea, is convinced that Oliver's going to steal the silver at the first opportunity. He challenges Brownlow to let Oliver prove his honesty by taking some books and a £5 note back to the bookshop.

Nancy has made a special effort to look smart and is hugely miffed when, near Brownlow's house, she is taken for what she is – a prostitute. Convinced she won't have the mettle to kidnap Oliver, Bill Sikes lurks in the background with his bulldog, when Oliver emerges from the house.

Oliver doesn't stand a chance, and the eerie shadows of Fagin's den close round him once more.

far left: Brownlow's aunt Mrs Bedwin (Annette Crosbie) carries in the water for the first hot bath Oliver has ever had in his life.

above: Oliver simply can't believe the luxury. He's a complete stranger to proper soap and hot water. It's a proper fire as well. Czech builders don't mess about with effects fires. They build a proper hearth out of brick, with an aluminium flue that snakes 30 feet up to the roof of the studio.

Episode Four

Wherein Oliver is delivered over to Mr William Sikes

The Master of the Workhouse has died, and Mrs Mann and Mr Bumble decide to get married. Mr Bumble calls it an 'opportunity for a joining of hearts and housekeepings!' but we strongly suspect it's a match of hell and high-water.

Monks wants to know how Fagin got Oliver back; Fagin wants to know when he's going to get his £600. Problems all round: Brownlow must see Oliver disgraced, but Oliver – currently locked in a dark room to ponder the perils of being good – is showing no signs of being bullied into a life of crime. Fagin's resolution is to have Bill Sikes and Toby Crackitt rob Brownlow's country house in Chertsey, taking Oliver along as the fall-guy. It's Crackitt who learns about the existence of the country house, after visiting Brownlow to tell him that Oliver is an imposter and a dyed-in-the-wool thief. Brownlow believes him.

As surety for the £600, Monks has given Fagin the ten-year-old letter from Leeford to Agnes. The letter contains a reference to the proof of Oliver's parentage: namely the locket containing the portraits of Agnes and Leeford. But Monks still has to find the locket itself.

Mrs Leeford visits Brownlow to collect her annual stipend. Half decrepit, half magnificent, she's also pretty convinced that she's about to get her hands on some real money: Oliver's inheritance. She needs sticks to support herself now but, being Mrs Leeford, she finds an alternative use for them. She smacks Brownlow on the head with one of them and declares that 'Bad as I am... I would rather be me, than you.'

opposite: Flash Toby Crackitt (Andrew Schofield) on his way to Brownlow's house. According to a contemporary report, burglars of his type 'have the look of sharp businessmen. They commit burglaries at country mansions, and sometimes at shops and warehouses, often extensive, and generally contrive to get away safely with their booty.' (Well, they would, wouldn't they?) They also 'regale themselves luxuriously on the choicest wines, and are lavish with their gold. From their superior manner and dress few would detect their real character. One might pass them daily in the street and not be able to recognise them.'

Alan Bleasdale's Toby is true to type; described in the stage directions as 'a far superior thief to Bill Sikes' and someone who 'laughs at his own verbal brilliance'.

this page: Brownlow's 'missing person' announcement and award for information about Oliver.

In the Chertsey house, Rose Fleming has returned from being 'finished' in Paris. She and Losberne, the handsome local doctor, are courting. At the same time, Fagin and Toby Crackitt are casing the joint and discover it to be full of treasures, and perfect for Oliver's downfall – especially as the only way they can get in is through a boy-sized window. When they return to London, Nancy is horrified to discover that Bill is determined to make Oliver's decline irreversible: Bill resolves that Oliver won't be seen alive again.

On the trail of the locket, Monks has returned to the seaside town and runs into Bumble in the local pub. Mrs Mann has emasculated him and he's not a happy Bumble. Yet he bucks up a bit when Monks informs him about the history of the locket he's searching for. Rifling through his wife's drawers Bumble has already located it. He later persuades her – without difficulty – that they should sell it to Monks for £30.

In Chertsey, the household has retired for the night and Bill Sikes, Toby Crackitt and Oliver make their move. Sikes and Crackitt, however, are sailing three sheets to the wind, and their drunken noises wake two of Brownlow's servants. The hapless Oliver has made it into the house – only to be shot and wounded by one of the servants. He lies bleeding and then the credits roll.

Monks (Marc Warren) finally gets his hands on the locket. Those bitten hands, like his scarred face, are a triumph of artistry. The make-up is 'Death Grey', the black wig covers naturally blond hair and the brown eye is a contact lens. But it's the way Marc Warren uses his hands that really impressed director Renny Rye. 'It's the first time I've ever cast a character on the strength of his knuckles...'

Episode Five

In which all is revealed…

No tea and sympathy for Oliver: Sikes and Crackitt scream at him to get up and stagger to the window. They haul him through and make their escape. But carrying Oliver impedes their progress. Sikes dumps him in a ditch and he and Crackitt run like hell. Brownlow's servants, Messrs Giles and Brittles, make a complete hash of giving chase, fail to see Oliver in the ditch and retire to the house to regale Cook with stories of their bravery.

Mrs Leeford and Monks sense victory via the locket that they've now bought from Mrs Mann and Bumble, and the latter goes to Fagin's den to deliver the good news. But Fagin is fuming over bad news: Toby Crackit has returned to report disaster – and Bill Sikes is missing. Now both Monks and Fagin are desperate men: Oliver, yet again, may be in a position to reveal all he knows to Brownlow.

He is. He has managed to stagger to the Chertsey house, is hidden there by Mrs Bedwin, and the goodly Dr Losberne is called upon to patch him up. This also provides Losberne and Rose with an unexpected flirting opportunity, and they make the most of it. Brownlow then arrives from London and discovers that Oliver is hidden in the house. Far from being angry, he's actually rather pleased. He never really did believe that Oliver was a criminal. Later, Rose ponders over how to entertain Oliver. She decides she'll teach him to play chess. 'Will anyone get hurt?' asks Oliver.

Bill Sikes, even more unkempt than usual, makes his way back to his lair in Bethnal Green. Nancy realises that Bill will not let Oliver give him the slip for a third time, but will now hunt him down and kill him. She makes a clandestine visit to Brownlow's house to tell all – but is distraught to discover that Brownlow isn't at home.

In Chertsey. Losberne asks Brownlow for Rose's hand and is refused. He reminds Brownlow too much of the handsome but feckless Leeford, and he doesn't want history repeating itself. Yet a different, crueller kind of history is repeating itself in the drawing room. The game of chess is interrupted by Monks and Fagin appearing at the window. Both Rose and Oliver are terrified: Rose by the face that 'came for Agnes' ten years previously, and Oliver by Fagin.

Fagin realises that he's now in very serious trouble. He hadn't a clue that there would be someone in the Chertsey house who could identify Monks. Now, if Rose, Oliver and Brownlow thrash out everything they know, they'll discover the extent of Fagin's involvement in the whole affair. Fagin determines to make himself scarce and abandon the den; lock, stock and stolen goods. He and the gang move to the filthy riverside area of Jacob's Island, and he pays a visit to Bill and Nancy to inform them of the fact. He's suspicious about Nancy's repeated refrains about needing 'a breath of fresh air', and deputes Charley Bates and The Artful Dodger to keep an eye on her.

this page: Bumble reduced to a shuffling, decrepit wreck outside the Workhouse. This time the snow is real. It added unscripted atmosphere to this scene – but nearly ruined the one filmed earlier that morning: one that was supposed to be shot in summer ten years previously.

opposite: Brownlow and Oliver on their way to Fagin's cell at Newgate Prison. It's actually not a prison and it's nowhere near Newgate – it's the grain store of the Czech monastery.

Cut to Monks and his mother. The full weight of the disaster sinks in to Mrs Leeford. She realizes they will never be able to extricate Oliver from Mr Brownlow; never get their hands on his inheritance. Raddled with alcohol and riddled with arthritis, she now has nothing left to live for. A pathetic and sad old woman, she shuffles off her mortal coil over, appropriately, a decanter of wine.

The Chertsey household decamp to London and Nancy pays them a visit. Her worries about Oliver are assuaged when she sees him alive and well, but Brownlow presses her to tell everything she knows about the man who wanted Oliver destroyed. Her description fits Monks and, having secretly followed Fagin to his home, she knows where he lives. Then, spurning Brownlow's offer of sanctuary, she departs. But Charley and Artful have followed her to the house and realise she has 'peached' on them all. Charley can't bring himself to snitch on her in return – but Artful can. He tells Bill Sikes what she's done. Bill's violent, complex yet, in its way, loving relationship with Nancy comes to an end. He murders her.

Losberne and Brownlow trace Monks to his rooms above The Three Cripples, and he leads them to Fagin's den – only to find it deserted. The hunt for Fagin begins, and with it the search for Bill. Charley Bates, who was once taken in by Brownlow, stole a clock from him and has been plagued by a guilty conscience ever since, has snitched on Bill. The police are now looking for a big, burly man attached to a faithful bulldog.

Fagin and Bill's mutual hatred erupts and they won't let one go down without the other. Bill falls to his death during a rooftop chase. Fagin thinks he's safe – but he has reckoned without Charley Bates' conscience. Charley 'peaches' on him, and he is arrested.

Back at Brownlow's house, the final pieces of the puzzle that is Oliver's life fall into place. Mrs Mann and Mr Bumble are called in to explain their part in the sorry saga. Predictably, they blame each other for the stealing and selling of the locket. Bumble hopes that these 'unfortunate, small events' (that would be armed robbery, murder and the selling of a child's soul) will not deprive him of his office. They do – in a big way. He and Mrs Mann end up as inmates of the Workhouse.

Monks repents and is forgiven. Brownlow and Oliver visit Fagin in Newgate Prison before his execution, and manage to retrieve the letter that Leeford wrote to Agnes. Oliver is finally and forever reunited with his family – a family who, in the final scene, celebrate the marriage of Rose and Losberne.

Nicholas Nickleby

The Old Curiosity Shop

Barnaby Rudge

Martin Chuzzlewit

A Christmas Carol

Dombey and Son

David Copperfield

Bleak House

Little Dorrit

A Tale of Two Cities

Great Expectations

Our Mutual Friend

The Mystery of Edwin Drood

David H A The

chapter 7

Charles Dickens

Dickens' staggering popularity, both at home and abroad, was unmatched by any other author of the age. In millions of words over thousands of pages he captured the very essence of the nineteenth century; it was his peculiar genius to represent more aspects of the national character than any contemporary (or indeed successor) succeeded in doing. His death in 1870 marked, literally, the end of an era – and not just in the country of his birth. In America, William Longfellow wrote that 'I never knew an author's death to cause such general mourning. It is no exaggeration to say that this whole country is stricken with grief'.

But if the greatest chronicler of his age was gone, his characters – almost two thousand of them – lived on. They still do; glittering testaments to a writer whose appeal remains universal. Yet Dickens' fiction was at the same time deeply personal – and the themes that appear in *Oliver Twist* and recur again and again in his fiction reveal almost as much about Dickens as they do about his times. He was credited – and indeed he credited himself – with an astonishing memory of childhood and even infancy. In an essay penned in later life, he wrote that 'it would be difficult to overstate the intensity and accuracy of an intelligent child's observation. At that impressible (sic) time of life, it must sometimes produce a fixed impression. If the fixed impression be of an object terrible to the child it will be (for want of reasoning upon) inseparable from great fear.'

From an early age, Dickens feared poverty – a direct result of his father's incarceration for debt in Marshalsea Prison. There are shades of those prison walls throughout Dickens' fiction and, crucially, there are children assuming responsibility for penurious adults. So too the themes of wills and legacies are constants in Dickens (because of his father's imprisonment, the young Dickens became acquainted with the Insolvent Debtors Act and the effect of money – or the lack of – on children). It's these inheritances that provide the timeless, dual themes of money and intrigue that drive the plots of so many of his novels. It's easy to forget that they - not chance or misfortune – propel Oliver Twist into the contrasting worlds of Fagin and Brownlow. For Dickens *was* a man in a hurry when he wrote the novel; he *did* reveal Oliver's background in a brief six pages (he wrote the last six chapters in three weeks), and this was, effectively, his first novel. He was only twenty-five when he wrote it – but he was already being hailed as one of the greatest writers of his century.

Charles John Huffham Dickens was born in 1812 in Portsmouth, the second of the eight children of John Dickens, a clerk in the Navy. He spent the happiest part of his childhood in Chatham (probably the model for the seaside town where Oliver Twist is born, and sometimes referred to as 'the wickedest place in the world'). When he was eleven the family moved to London, and met with financial disaster. John Dickens, who rarely managed to live within his income, was arrested and was incarcerated with his family in Marshalsea Debtors' Prison. Only Charles remained at liberty. A relative, aware of the looming disaster, had offered him work at a blacking warehouse – labelling bottles for six shillings a week – and separate lodgings had been found for him. Here, then, are the memories that lodged so firmly in the mind of the young Dickens and that influenced so much of his fiction – in particular the early chapters of *David Copperfield* (1849-50) and *Little Dorrit* (1855-57).

The family spent three months in prison and after their release Charles was removed from work and sent to school. He was bright – very bright – but his formal education ended at fifteen when he began work as an office boy, later studying shorthand and becoming a reporter in the Commons. He soon gained a reputation for speed and accuracy, and his first *Sketches by Boz* (a pseudonym he maintained until the publication of *Oliver Twist*) began to appear in various magazines shortly after his twenty-first birthday. They attracted widespread attention, and led to a commission by publishers Chapman and Hall to provide text to accompany illustrations by the artist Seymour. Thus was born Mr Pickwick, and the publication, in twenty monthly instalments from 1836-37, of *The Posthumous Papers of the Pickwick Club*. After a slow start, the papers became fantastically popular and something of a cult.

The astonishing speed at which Dickens wrote enabled him to begin *Oliver Twist* whilst still producing the *Pickwick Papers* – and to begin *Nicholas Nickleby* before *Oliver Twist* was competed. To a large extent, *Oliver Twist* was his first novel, as origins of the *Pickwick Papers* lay with others. Again published in monthly instalments (as were all his novels), *Oliver Twist* appeared in 1837 in a new magazine, *Bentley's Miscellany*, of which Dickens was the first editor. By this time he had quit parliamentary reporting, and his future career as a writer largely depended on the success of *Oliver Twist*. It *was* successful, although critics, accustomed to the comedy of Pickwick, were surprised by the darker, more sombre tone. But it wasn't terribly well received in aristocratic circles. A certain Lady Carlisle remarked that 'I know there are such unfortunate beings as pickpockets and streetwalkers, but I do now much wish to hear what they say to one another.'

next page: Gad's Hill Place, near Rochester, Kent. Dickens died here and, as his biographer Peter Ackroyd writes, 'he had died in the house which he had first seen as a small boy and which his father had pointed out to him as a suitable object of his ambitions; so great was his father's hold upon his life that, forty years later, he had bought it.'

Dickens' subsequent novels were: *Nicholas Nickleby* (1838-9); *The Old Curiosity Shop* (1840-1); *Barnaby Rudge* (1841); *Martin Chuzzlewit* (1843-4); *A Christmas Carol* (1843); *Dombey and Son* (1846-8); *David Copperfield* (1849-50); *Bleak House* (1852-3); *Hard Times* (1854); *Little Dorrit* (1855-7); *A Tale of Two Cities* (1859); *Great Expectations* (1860-1); *Our Mutual Friend* (1864-5). He died before completing his last novel, *The Mystery of Edwin Drood* (1870).

Dickens was staggeringly, almost stupefyingly prolific. As well as his novels, he continued to write journalism throughout his career, he travelled widely (latterly delivering a series of readings in America and the provinces), he produced and took leading roles in amateur dramatics, found time for philanthropic enterprises, for social reform, for his family (he and his wife, Catherine Hogarth, produced ten children) and for a vast circle of friends.

In his will he wrote that 'I emphatically direct that I be buried in an inexpensive, unostentatious and strictly private manner... I conjure my friends on no account to make me the subject of any monument, memorial or testimonial whatever.'

They didn't. They didn't need to – the only monuments that could possibly do justice to Dickens had already been created.